Contents

Acknowledgements   iv
Series introduction   v

Part 1   Introduction and overview

1 What is sociological research?   1
2 Microsociology and macrosociology   9

Part 2   Methods in sociology

3 Science and sociology   17
4 Quantitative research: surveys   31
5 Qualitative research: observation   43
6 Evaluating sociological research   57
7 Research, values and objectivity   68

Part 3   Statistical data and documentary readings

8   Statistics   75
9   Theories, values and research   83
10 Research methods   91
11 Projects in methodology   102

Further r   107
Index   110

Acknowledgements

I would like to especially thank Pat Madden for reading the manuscript of this book at various stages, and providing a lot of useful comments. I am grateful also to Joy Outten for providing much needed help with typing. And special thanks to my mother, Glenys Morison, for preparing the index so quickly and expertly.

We are grateful to the following for permission to reproduce copyright material:

Aldine Publishing Co for an extract from *The Discovery of Grounded Theory* by Barney G Glaser & Anselm L Strauss (New York: Aldine Pub Co) Copyright (c) 1967 A L Strauss & B G Glaser; Harper & Row Publishers Inc for an extract from *Sociology: Traditional & Radical Perspectives* by H J Sherman & J Wood (1982); Longman Group Ltd for extracts from *Data Collection in Context* by Ackroyd & Hughes (1981); the author's agents for an extract from *Managers & Their Wives* by J M & R E Pahl (1971); Routledge & Kegan Paul plc for an extract from *Doing Feminist Research* ed Helen Roberts (1981); the author's agents for an extract from *Working Class Childhood* by J Seabrook.

SOCIOLOGY IN FOCUS SERIES
General Editor: Murray Morison

UNIVERSITY OF
GLOUCESTERSHIRE
at Cheltenham and Gloucester

LONGMAN GROUP UK LIMITED
*Longman House, Burnt Mill, Harlow, Essex CM20 2JE, UK
and Associated Companies throughout the World.*

**Published in the United States of America
by Longman Inc., New York**

© **Longman Group Limited 1986**
*All rights reserved; no part of this publication
may be reproduced, stored in a retrieval system,
or transmitted in any form or by any means, electronic,
mechanical, photocopying, recording, or otherwise,
without either the prior written permission of the Publishers
or a licence permitting restricted copying issued by
the Copyright Licensing Agency Ltd,
90 Tottenham Court Road, London W1P 9HE.*

*First published 1986
Eleventh impression 1994*

ISBN 0 582 35507 9

Set in 10/11 pt Bembo, Linotron 202

Printed in Malaysia by TCP

British Library Cataloguing in Publication Data

Morison, Murray
    Methods in sociology. — (Sociology in focus series)
    1. Sociology — Methodology
    I. Title   II. Series
301'.01'8   HM24

ISBN 0-582-35507-9

Library of Congress Cataloguing in Publication Data

Morison, Murray
    Methods in sociology.
    (Sociology in focus series)
    Bibliography: p.
    Includes index.
    1. Sociology. 2. Sociology — Methodology.
    I. Title   II. Series
HM51.M734 1985   301'.01'8   85–13273
ISBN 0–582–35507–9

*The publisher's policy is to use paper manufactured
from sustainable forests.*

Series introduction

Sociology in Focus aims to provide an up-to-date, coherent coverage of the main topics that arise on an introductory course in sociology. While the intention is to do justice to the intricacy and complexity of current issues in sociology, the style of writing has deliberately been kept simple. This is to ensure that the student coming to these ideas for the first time need not become lost in what can appear initially as jargon.

Each book in the series is designed to show something of the purpose of sociology and the craft of the sociologist. Throughout the different topic areas the interplay of theory, methodology and social policy have been highlighted, so that rather than sociology appearing as an unwieldy collection of facts, the student will be able to grasp something of the process whereby sociological understanding is developed. The format of the books is broadly the same throughout. Part one provides an overview of the topic as a whole. In part two the relevant research is set in the context of the theoretical, methodological and policy issues. The student is encouraged to make his or her own assessment of the various arguments, drawing on the statistical and reference material provided both here and at the end of the book. The final part of the book contains both statistical material and a number of 'Readings'. Questions have been provided in this section to direct students to analyse the materials presented in terms of both theoretical assumptions and methodological approaches. It is intended that this format should enable students to exercise their own sociological imaginations rather than to see sociology as a collection of universally accepted facts, which just have to be learned.

While each book in the series is complete within itself, the similarity of format ensures that the series as a whole provides an integrated and balanced introduction to sociology. It is intended that the text can be used both for individual and classroom study, while the inclusion of the variety of statistical and documentary materials lend themselves to both the preparation of essays and brief seminars.

Dedication
For Gill

PART 1
Introduction and overview

1 What is sociological research?

Jimmy Boyle, who was a violent gang leader in Glasgow in the 1960s, describes how his gang came to change its name:

> Around this time the 'Wild Young Cumbie' were very active, getting involved in lots of heavy fighting scenes and were getting the name of being the best fighting gang ever to come out of the Gorbals, both collectively and as individuals. Some of them were involved in a big fight that was reminiscent of a wild west saloon brawl in the Gorbals and there was a big court trial afterwards where John McCue, Artie Austin and three others were involved, and all given sentences. John – 4 years and Artie – 18 months. The Press made a big deal of it and labelled John as the leader. The fact was that another guy was the leader. This was all part of the image building process of the Press. All of us younger kids would pore over these newspapers and the press coverage only confirmed the years of adulation that we had given them. Being in the papers was a great thing to us. All the kids that went about with me, idolised these guys so when they were jailed and put out of the way we saw fit to change the name of our gang from the 'Skull' to the 'Cumbie'. Our activities on the gang scene became more intense.
>
> Jimmy Boyle, *A Sense of Freedom*, Pan Books 1977

Boyle gives an autobiographical account in his book, of his time in a gang, and in prison. Is this sociology? To answer this question we will need to know more about what constitutes sociology and what are the research methods used by sociologists. The purpose of this book is to describe and explain the variety of methods that sociologists use in their research.

We can contrast Boyle's book with that of the sociologist James Patrick. He spent time with a Glasgow gang participating in their activities. Here is part of his description of the gang 'just dossin' aw day':

> Life with the gang was not all violence, sex and petty delinquency. Far from it. One of the foremost sensations that remains with me is the feeling of unending boredom, of crushing tedium, of listening hour after hour at street corners to desultory conversation and indiscriminate grumbling. Standing with one's back against the wall, with one's hands in one's pockets, in the late afternoon, and in the early hours of the morning, was *the* gang activity. At times I longed to discard my passive role and suggest some constructive form of entertainment. Once, I remember, we were all slouching against the walls of 'wir corner' when it began to drizzle. No one made any move to seek the protection of a close-mouth or a shop-front and so, in my observer status, I had to stand there and let the rain trickle down my face.
>
> Some boys whispered and at least some snatches of their conversation provided me with valuable information ... Others had no interest even in talking, and were content to let their minds go blank. Smoking, chewing gum, recounting past exploits, deriding passers by, and indulging in horse-play with each other and with the girls, these were the only diversions from 'dossin'. Neither the young nor the old escaped their caustic and obscene abuse. Specifically delinquent activities occupied only a small fraction of their waking hours.
>
> James Patrick, *A Glasgow Gang Observed,* Eyre Methuen 1973

Patrick's account is a result of participant observation. He was able to join in some of the gang's activities because of his contact with Tim, a gang member. He was teaching in an approved school where he had met Tim. Tim had wanted to show him 'whit the score wis' with the gang, and what they did.

In each of these examples we are gaining some insight into the life of the delinquent and his outlook. Although one account is written by a sociologist and the other is not, there is a certain similarity. To decide how far each can be considered to be 'good sociology' we would need to know more about how the information in each case was derived. Before considering this we will look at a very different type of information. This is provided by official statistics, in this case the number of indictable offences (serious crimes) committed by teenage boys. These Home Office figures would seem to indicate a sharp increase in the number of offences being committed (see Fig. 1.1).

Figure 1.1 Boys 14–17 years – indictable offences (Data from Home Office)

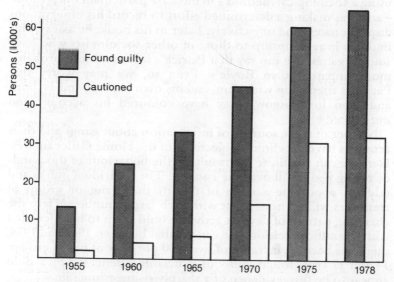

While these statistics have been collected from the courts and prepared by the Home Office, they are obviously of considerable interest to sociologists who are studying delinquency. Here seem to be some 'hard facts' for the sociologist to go on, and to seek to explain. We shall see though that the 'facts' are not so certain as they appear to be at first, when we look at the methods used to collect the information.

Let us look at the types of information that have come from the three sources we have examined so far. With Jimmy Boyle we have an account of life of a 'hard man' from Glasgow, written while he is in prison serving a life sentence for murder. If we are going to use this material as sociologists we will want to ask some questions about it. Is his account accurate? How selective is he being? Is he covering up some things so we will think better of him? Even if he is not, how far can his memory be trusted? We would have to conclude that while Boyle may give a good description from his viewpoint, he did not use any rigorous methods of research in collecting his data. He is only drawing on his own experience.

With James Patrick we also have an account of one man's experience, but with a major difference. He was consciously using a sociological method – in this case participant observation – and was making a determined effort to record his observations dispassionately and objectively. Later in his book, he assesses his findings in relationship to those of other sociologists who have studied gangs. We can say that Patrick's information is probably more impartial than Boyle's. Even so, we may worry that Patrick's friendship with Tim, and his own background as 'born and bred in Glasgow' may have coloured his account and introduced bias.

Neither of these sources of information about gangs and their activities have the clinical objectivity of the Home Office figures. Here we can scrutinise the results of the behaviour of thousands of young people all over the country. The individual quirks and oddities about the actions of this or that gang or group of teenagers will be ironed out with such large numbers. Here the changing pattern of deviant activity would seem to be calculated with scientific precision. We can say that between 1964 and 1978, there has been an increase of over 500 per cent of boys between 14 and 17 years found guilty of indictable offences. This would appear to be firm evidence of a sharply rising crime rate.

Yet as sociologists we will have to ask searching questions about how reliable these statistics actually are. We will want to look at the way in which they were compiled. We may even suggest that to a certain extent these figures are really unreliable as a measure of delinquent behaviour, because the statistics may not accurately represent such behaviour (see Chapter 8).

While we may agree that these first three examples are all sociological to some extent, could we say the same of a novel? Particularly, would we say the same about a spy novel dealing with Palestinian terror and Israeli revenge? Consider the following quote:

'I would say exploitation is the crunch issue, Marty,' Litvak breathed. 'For exploitation read *property* and you have the whole bit. First the exploiter hits the wage slave over the head

with his superior wealth; then he brainwashes him into
believing that the pursuit of property is a valid motive for
breaking him at the grindstone. That way he has him hooked
twice over.'

John Le Carré, *The Little Drummer Girl*,
Hodder and Stoughton, 1983

Le Carré has given, through one of his characters, a compressed
account of a marxist analysis of private ownership, power and
exploitation. Does a novel which includes sociological concepts
constitute sociology? We would have to say no, because this is
incidental in a novel that investigates international terrorism.
However, international terrorism is of interest to sociologists.
When we look at Le Carré's introduction we find that he
undertook quite extensive research before writing his book. He
mentions some of his contacts, who included Israeli officers in
the intelligence service, and the chief of Israeli Military Intelligence. He also spoke to a Palestinian military commander, and
visited the Palestinian camps.

Of the Palestinians some are dead, others are taken prisoner,
the rest are presumably for the most part homeless or dis-
persed. The fighting boys who looked after me in the upper
flat in Sidon and chatted with me in the tangerine groves; the
bomb-weary but indomitable refugees of the camps at Rashi-
diyeh and Nabatiyeh: from what I hear, their fate is very little
different from that of their reconstructed counterparts in this
story.

Le Carré, *The Little Drummer Girl*

While we would have to acknowledge the limitations, novels
that have been thoroughly researched may indeed be of some
value to sociologists. They may occasionally help to inform
sociological debate and deepen understanding.

We will look next at the process of researching into society
and generating sociological knowledge, and try to establish what
it is that makes certain approaches to understanding society
sociological.

Making sense of society

All members of society have to try and make sense of what is
going on around them. We all have some vague idea about the

community and society which we live in, and how to operate within it. We all have a common sense grasp of the social reality of which we are part.

Chris Brown, in the opening part of his useful book on sociological theory, describes how he gets his new students to 'draw a picture or a diagram which represents "society"'. Most find this exercise easy, producing circles, or triangle shapes, or groups of little 'stick-men' and so on. Although society is an abstract concept, a system of invisible interrelationships and interactions, we seem to have undertaken no specific research, nor even read any if we are only starting out on a sociology course, yet we can come up with a 'model' of society.

We could call these internal models that we have of various aspects of our social world our 'understanding of the social world'. In everyday life we do not have to think much about it, when dealing with the bus conductor, getting information from a telephone operator or understanding what is meant by the term 'housewife'. Things become less easy if we move into a situation which is unfamiliar. Going to a new school or college, starting a job, going on a package holiday with strangers or visiting a family from a different ethnic background to your own; all require coping with the new and the unfamiliar. Berger and Kellner put it this way:

> Following the distinctions made by Alfred Schutz, two broad kinds of meanings may be distinguished: there are the meanings within the individual's own life-world, those that are actually or potentially 'within reach' or 'at hand', and that are usually self-understood in the natural attitude of everyday living. And then there are the meanings *outside* the individual's own life-world, meanings of other societies or less familiar sectors of one's own society, also meanings from the past.
>
> Berger and Kellner, *Sociology Reinterpreted*, Penguin 1982

When we accommodate to a new situation or the point of view of another, then our own viewpoint changes a bit. As Berger and Kellner say: 'I cannot interpret another's meaning, without changing, albeit minimally, my own meaning system'. We sum up the argument developed so far, in Fig. 1.2. The familiar social world 'out there' we represent with our understanding, or social theories. To make sense of less familiar worlds we may have to change or adjust our misunderstanding.

Figure 1.2

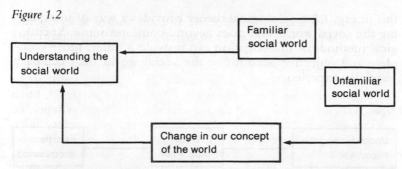

What we have said up to this point applies to all individuals undergoing the universal process of socialisation. However, as Berger and Kellner point out 'there is a difference between the ordinary interpretation of meanings in everyday life and the interpretation of social science'. Using the methods of social science and drawing on the variety of types of explanations of social processes and activities, the social scientist can, in a sense, see further, or see deeper into the nature of society.

An example will help make this clearer. The ordinary person in the street probably believes that newspapers mainly report the news in a reasonably unbiased way. They would be surprised by the notion that they may 'create the news' as well. Yet by applying some of the concepts of 'labelling theory', some sociologists have investigated the role of newspapers in creating street violence and drug cultures. By using interviews, participant observation and documentary research, sociologists like Stan Cohen and Jock Young have shown that the common sense view about part of the social world – in this case newspapers – is inadequate, and *masking* in a sense, an 'unfamiliar social world' where the *latent functions* of some of the newspapers can be shown to be the creating of certain reactions by the police, or 'moral panics' by the public.

Merton, an influential American sociologist, spoke of *manifest functions,* which refer to the officially defined purposes of a particular social institution and *latent functions* which are the underlying or less obvious purposes. It is these which the sociologist may uncover, demonstrating, as Berger and Kellner point out, that 'the world is not what it appears to be'. This seeing in a more penetrating way involves both drawing on sociological theory, and using research methods. We represent this in Fig. 1.3. Sociological theory provides a way of interpreting the social world that goes beyond common sense. Sociological methods of investigation can provide a fuller, more complete and objective account of the social world than ordinary 'everyday experience'.

Figure 1.3

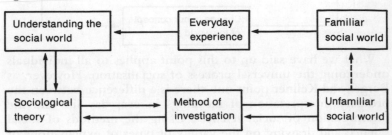

We can conclude this part of the discussion by attempting to define what sociological methodology involves. There are three aspects that are touched on in this book:

1 a way of understanding and explaining society – *theory*
2 a way of investigating society – *methodology*
3 a way of using the information acquired – *action taken* or *social policy*

The last aspect, which will often determine the reason *why* the research was carried out, may well reflect the values of the researcher. The problem of value freedom and objectivity will be looked at in detail. It will be a major theme of this book that the current theories, values and interests of researchers affect *all* scientific endeavour. This problem of prejudice and clouding of vision, which affect common sense views of the world even more than those of social scientists, is considered in detail in Chapter 9. Most of the space in this book will be given over to investigating the variety of methods sociologists use. However, the process of generating sociological knowledge cannot be divorced from social theory, and this is what we will briefly turn to next.

2 Microsociology and macrosociology

Sociologists approach their study of society and social issues in a variety of ways. In this chapter we are concerned with one of the broad divisions of the sociological approach between those whose interest is with the smaller units of society, particularly with the way people make sense of their social situation, and those who direct their attention to the whole of society. This concern with meanings on the one hand and structure on the other, tends to involve different methodologies.

Microsociology

Microsociology is concerned with the small scale, the 'close-up' view of society. The sociologist directs his or her attention to one aspect of social activity or one group or small scale institution. We have already considered Patrick's study of one gang. This is microsociology because although the phenomenon of the gang and gangs in general, may well be a part of larger scale social factors like poverty, social deprivation, working class sub-cultures or whatever, it will not necessarily tell us anything definitive about those 'structural factors'. Instead we are provided with an analysis of the workings of a gang, rich in detail but limited in scope. David Hargreaves' study of a secondary modern school (1967), which showed the effect that streaming had on the development of pro- and anti-school attitudes by the pupils, provides another example. His work was based on one school which he both taught in and studied. His findings highlight how organisational features may influence the development of certain attitudes and patterns of behaviour.

In studies like these concepts such as class, culture and power, which relate to society as a whole, may play a part in the analysis. However the focus remains on the small scale rather than the vast structures and institutions of society. We would expect that microsociological concerns will tend to involve a different type of research to those of macrosociology.

Macrosociology

Karl Marx sought to do nothing less than to explain the origins of modern industrial capitalist society. His concern was not with the minutiae of social processes but with the broad canvas of the whole of society. Indeed he encompassed in his theories the different types of society, from tribal societies right up to the complex industrial societies of nineteenth century Europe and beyond to the predicted communist societies of the future. In his analysis the vast class structures in society took a central place, particularly the great divisions between the group that owned the means of making a livelihood (whether land or factories), and those who had to work for them (farm workers or factory workers).

Max Weber, who did not agree with Marx's analysis, was still concerned with society as a whole. One of his most famous studies attempted to demonstrate that changes in religious thought had been a crucial factor influencing the growth of modern capitalism. To demonstrate this he compared in detail, the societies of India, China and Europe.

Other writers who approach society on the macro-scale would include marxists like Bourdieu and Althusser, as well as functionalists like Parsons. We suggest that the *type* of research that is undertaken by sociologists will tend to vary according to whether their approach is one of macrosociology or microsociology. We will look at this next.

Qualitative research

With qualitative research the 'texture' and 'feel' of the social situation becomes the centre of attention. What does being in the gang *mean* to the participant? What is it *like* to be an inmate of an asylum? How does a coroner come to *define* certain deaths as 'suicide' and others as not? With qualitative research the sociologist cannot make the same claims to objectivity as those doing quantitative research, because he or she is seeking to experience or understand the more subjective viewpoint of the actor in the social situation. The value of this research lies in its attempt to view the world through the eyes of those being studied. It cannot be considered scientific in the normal sense of that term.

This approach to sociology, using various forms of participant observation and unstructured interviews, has been very influential in the last few decades. The sheer richness, perception and originality of work in this more interpretive tradition has made sociologists question whether they should always be trying to emulate the hard statistical basis of the natural sciences.

We will look next at one example of this type of research that used participant observation as the main research technique.

Researching spoonbending

The impact on public interest of the apparent powers of Uri Geller in the early 1970s, was considerable. All over the country children were claiming to be able to bend spoons and keys, in a manner similar to Geller's. The scientific community was very sceptical of these powers to say the least. It was assumed that Geller was a magician and a charlatan, interested in money and publicity. Certain scientists decided to investigate the phenomena and to study the children who appeared to have developed these extraordinary powers.

Two sociologists, Collins and Pinch, joined the team of scientists researching these possible powers, as scientists. In other words they participated fully as scientists, rather than just observing in some other capacity. However, they also carried out their own sociological research.

Their special position as sociologist scientists gave them a view of the operation of a scientific research project, in a way that could not have been achieved by just carrying out interviews with scientists after the event. For one thing they would not necessarily have known all the relevant questions to ask; for another, the scientists might not remember accurately what had taken place, or even have fully realised all that was going on at the time. Their work can be considered as microsociology because it focuses in on one particular social situation. Being so closely involved in the scientific work revealed to them many of the influences that affected research into spoonbending (and by implication other similar research into parapsychology). The media provided a constant pressure for unambiguous results. They experienced sharp criticism from other scientists and this perhaps explained why the media were used as an outlet for publishing findings. Collins describes how they observed that there was a subtle pressure on the scientists to interpret ambiguous results as null results, rather than to see them as giving examples of children having paranormal powers. He goes on:

Though resistance to fringe science has been well documented in the literature, the subtle permeability to outside pressure of day to day laboratory observation would be difficult to understand without experiencing it. Other pay-offs which can be documented easily include the experiences of interaction with the media, with the subjects of the experiments and with scientific colleagues. All these experiences, which emerged from our role as experimenters rather than as observers, presented surprises to us in the form of unexpected pressures to act one way rather than another. For example, the media demanded black and white findings irrespective of whether they were positive or negative. The lure of the media both in terms of financial reward and flattery was especially highlighted by the astonishing vituperativeness of colleagues who had no idea of what we were up to except that it had to do with the paranormal. This reaction helped us to realise how much the academic relies on support from colleagues in the normal way, and helps explain the undignified flirtations with the media that parapsychologists occasionally engage in – it may be the only form of recognition left for a parascientist . . . The lack of subtlety in the war between the parapsychologists and their critics needed to be experienced to be believed.

> H.M. Collins, 'Researching Spoonbending', in *Social Researching: Politics, Problems and Practice,* edited by Colin Bell and Helen Roberts, Routledge and Kegan Paul, 1984

There are few general laws or principles that can emerge from a study like this that can be said to apply to society as a whole. Here the concentration is on why the scientists behave the way they do, seen from the point of view of the scientists themselves. This micro-approach involving a handful of people contrasts with their research into much larger numbers, which we will now consider.

Quantitative research

Quantitative research, as the name suggests, involves description and data presented in numerical form. Such research follows the scientific method as far as possible, in as much as it attempts to accurately and objectively measure social factors. The results of the Census, and the more detailed General Household Survey, fall into this category, for they provide information on income, housing, family size, ownership of cars, fridges, telephones etc. The techniques associated with quantitative research involve social surveys, postal questionnaires, interviews, computerised analysis of results and so on.

The extensive studies of social mobility by both Glass (1954) and Goldthorpe and Halsey with the Oxford Mobility Study (1980), present their complex statistical models in the context of the social class structure. Both pieces of research involved studying thousands of men and plotting their movements up and down the class hierarchy. In their tables and statistics, an objective picture of changes in class structure is presented. The various factors that may influence social mobility and indeed many other aspects of social life and life changes have been extensively researched in a study quite remarkable for its scope, which we now turn to.

Born to Fail?

The opportunity to follow a very large number of children throughout their childhood and into adulthood, would provide the social scientist with a wealth of valuable information, that might have considerable implications for social policy. This opportunity came in 1958 with information being gathered on virtually all the children born in one week in March 1958, in England, Scotland and Wales. This provided a 'cohort' of 17,000 children at birth, who could be studied. The development of these children has been monitored through to adulthood, providing a rich and unique source of information on the 'normal' child as well as the 'abnormal'.

A study based on the children at age 11, by Wedge and Prosser, was called *Born to Fail* (1974). In it, those children defined as disadvantaged in terms of three factors, low income, poor housing, and family composition (one parent families or large families), were compared with the children who had no such disadvantage. The results were startlingly clear. Those disadvantaged in these environmental terms tended to be significantly lighter at birth, more prone to illness, have parents who were more likely to be out of work or ill. In each case the comparison between the two groups could be quantified, as with the need to share a bed (52.8 per cent of the disadvantaged, as compared to 9.2 per cent of the other children). In school they were less likely to do well in the key subjects of maths and English.

The virtue of a study like this is that it produces 'hard facts'. The thousands of children studied, drawn from all over the British Isles, means that the data is likely to be reliable. It provides a valid picture of child development which can form a sound basis for policy decisions. The results of surveys like this can be presented in numerical form. The data that is derived from such studies is scientific, in the sense that it is a sound description of a particular sample, from which we can confidently generalise to other similar groups.

It is clear that the qualitative and quantitative methods of research which tend to be associated with microsociology and macrosociology respectively, differ very considerably both in technique and the type of information or knowledge they produce. We will take a brief look at this next.

Social structure and social action

It is an important premise of this book that research methods cannot be divorced from theory. A piece of research has to be understood in the context of the general theoretical assumptions and orientations within which it takes place. It would not be appropriate to go into detail here about issues of theory but some discussion of the relationship between theoretical outlook and methodological practice will be necessary. At this point it will be helpful to clarify the distinction between the macrosociological concern with social structure and the microsociology of social action.

To borrow from Peter Berger, we could say that the structural approach to sociology tends to emphasise 'man in society' whereas the social action perspective would stress 'society in man'. The structural approach sees members of society as being

Figure 2.1

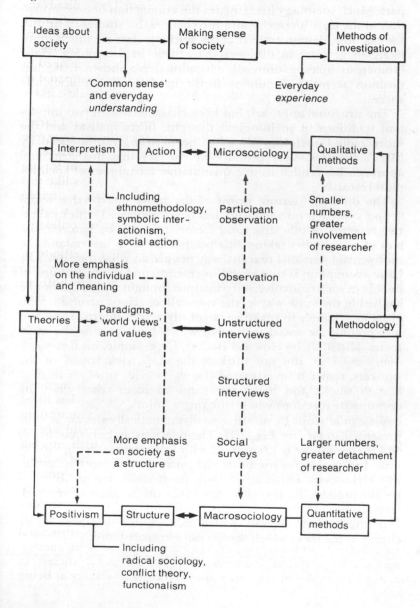

very much influenced by the social structure of which they are part. Much sociology investigates the connection between position in the class hierarchy and life chances. So studies of health, for example, demonstrate that the working class are much more likely to get certain illnesses than those in the middle class. Numerous investigations of education have shown that class position seems a dominant factor in determining academic success.

The structural approach has been characteristic of two important traditions in sociological thought, functionalism and the more radical sociology that has been strongly influenced by Marx's theories. Very broadly we can say that this structural approach has tended to use quantitative techniques of sociological research.

The different starting point of the more interpretive social action approach on sociology has been associated with qualitative research. While structural factors may not be ignored, the aim of sociologists taking this perspective is to understand the motives and personal reasons why people do what they do. The basic assumption is that social interaction and the operations of people in society involve selfconscious thought and so cannot be studied in the same way as the non-selfconscious natural world. How man comes to make sense of his world, internalising and interpreting the social system of which he is part, is the main focus. The study by Howard Becker, for example, on *Becoming a Marihuana User,* did not look at the class background of the smokers, rather it investigated the way novice smokers learned *how* to smoke and how they came to learn what were the appropriate reactions when smoking a 'joint'.

We can attempt to summarise diagramatically the arguments presented so far (see Fig. 2.1). The relationship between theory and methodology is presented, with interpretism being closely linked to qualitative methods and positivism to more quantitative techniques. However it must be stressed that sociologists employing specific theories may often use a range of research techniques.

In the analysis section which follows, we will look more closely at the ideas which are set out in the diagram.

PART 2

Methods in sociology

3 Science and sociology

What is science?

In the last 200 years or so we have seen an extraordinary advance
in scientific knowledge. Science has demonstrated that people
can predict and control nature to such an extent that they can
send spaceships to Saturn, undertake surgery with laser beams
and tap the energy at the heart of the atom. The power of the
natural sciences is evidence of their truth. A fundamental question for those studying society in any of its aspects, economic,
political, social or psychological, is whether they can be scientific in the same sense as the natural sciences.

Science can be defined in a number of ways. It derives from
the latin word *scire*, 'to know'. One definition could therefore be
that science is a *system of verifiable knowledge*. In other words it is
the organised knowledge that we have about something that we
are able to demonstrate is factually correct. A social survey into,
for example, people's incomes would fall into this category,
because a number of such surveys conducted under the same
conditions would produce very similar results.

Science can be given a more rigorous definition. This would
relate to the way in which scientific knowledge is gathered. In
the sixteenth century, Francis Bacon emphasised the great
importance of *empiricism*. Knowledge was to be built up from
what we could test with our senses, and of which, he argued, we
could be certain. This building up of knowledge from what we
experience is called the inductive method, and has been very
important in science. However, science involves more than just

Fig. 3.1 **The scientific method**
1 The scientist is confronted with a **problem** requiring explanation.
2 The scientist analyses the problem in the light of relevant **theory**.
3 From the theory, the scientist devides specific **hypotheses** to be tested.
4 Through **observation** or **experiment** the scientist tests out his or her hypothesis, using accurate **measurement**, under **controlled** conditions.
5 As a result, he or she obtains **data**.
6 The data is analysed to establish whether the hypothesis can be supported or refuted by the **fact** or **results**.
7 The hypothesis and theory are adjusted in the light of the results, and the findings are **published**.

careful observation and measurement. Often the scientist is testing out a theory that attempts to explain a particular problem that is confronting him or her. Science can therefore be defined as a method of *investigation* (see Fig. 3.1).

We need not explore all the detailed arguments about how modern science developed. However, it is worth noting that following the influence of Bacon, and the mathematician Descartes, it came to be accepted that the physical world is a bit like an extremely elaborate mechanical system that operates according to fixed laws. The purpose of science was to discover these laws. This was to be accomplished through the objective use of the scientific method.

Gradually, by applying this rigorous and carefully controlled method, the secrets of the universe might be unfolded. Modern science has clearly been very successful and, as a way of generating knowledge, has apparently proved its worth. It will be helpful at this stage to consider the way in which scientific knowledge is produced (see Fig. 3.2).

The belief in the certainty of scientific knowledge, and the idea of progress through science, was at its peak in the nineteenth century. This faith in the scientific method influenced early sociologists, who wished to establish sociology as a

Fig. 3.2 Science and 'ideas' about 'things'

All science involves an attempt to describe and explain some aspect of the world or of reality. Common sense and everyday experience tells us that there is something real 'out there' to be studied and understood. Any particular science is a system of ideas about that reality, that aids understanding and provides explanations. For example the science of genetics has developed elaborate ideas and theories about plants and animals. The application of this knowledge has demonstrated its apparent validity and truthfulness, by enabling new types of plants or breeds of animals to be developed.

There would appear, therefore, to be two fundamental aspects of science, first, the 'reality' being studied (ontology or being), second, the ideas and theories about this reality (epistemology or knowledge). Through a specific methodology the ideas about this reality can be tested and knowledge gained. For example in the case of the geneticist, this might be by experiments involving plant breeding.

We can summarise this idea with a diagram, that can clearly be related to Fig. 1.3 in Chapter 1 (page 8).

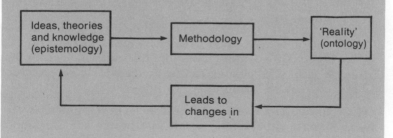

With sociology, the question is raised as to whether the nature of society has the same type of reality (ontology) as the material universe. Also, can the methodology of the sciences be used in a similar way in sociology, to provide knowledge (epistemology) that has the certainty of a natural science. (For a fuller discussion of this idea, see Bilton *et al.*, *Introductory Sociology*, Macmillan, 1981.)

science as well. The 'founding father' of sociology (he coined the word), Auguste Comte (1798–1857), argued that a science of society was possible, and that the laws of society would be discovered through the application of rational scientific principles. This view of the certainty of knowledge derived from using an objective scientific method, is called *positivism*.

Later, Emile Durkheim (1858–1917), an eminent and highly influential early sociologist, enshrined the positivist approach in his suggested rules for sociological enquiry. He argued that social phenomena, or 'social facts', could be treated as 'things'. They could therefore be measured in the same way as physical things.

Karl Marx (1818–1883), whose approach to the study of society was greatly at variance with that of Durkheim, nevertheless also believed in a positivistic science of sociology. He was convinced that societies changed according to clear laws, which could be objectively demonstrated.

We will return to the question of positivism, and the claim of sociology to be scientific, a little later in this chapter. We need first to consider the work of a contemporary philosopher of science, Karl Popper. He has suggested that scientific knowledge is more tentative than positivist scientists would have us believe. In fact he would argue that we can never be certain that a thing is true (see Fig. 3.3).

Popper is critical of some sociological theory, particularly that of Marx, and others like Herbert Spencer who take what Popper calls an 'historicist' position. These are theories which claim that the course of societal change can be predicted. He is critical for two main reasons, as summarised by Pratt (1978).

1 The evidence of a fixed pattern of social development is very weak because either there is only one case to act as evidence (i.e. the history of the societies being investigated) or if more cases are quoted, the differences between them are greater than their similarities.
2 The idea of predicting accurately how a society will develop is easily demonstrated to be false. We cannot know what will be invented in the future (for if we did it would have been invented already). However, such inventions (like the steam engine or the splitting of the atom) profoundly affect society. Future inventions would seem likely to have far reaching, but unpredictable, consequences.

Fig. 3.3 Conjectures and refutations
Karl Popper has been very influential in the debate over
what the scientific method can be and ought to be. He
suggests that when a scientist is seeking to understand or to
explain anything he uses theories (conjectures) which are
ideas about *why* things are occurring the way they are.
While he is a tough critic of empiricism, or the belief that
knowledge about the world comes only through sensory
experience, he emphasises the need for thorough empirical
investigation of any theories held. The hypothesis a scientist uses must, he argues, be testable. More than this, it
must be possible to prove them wrong (refutation).

It is not enough for experiments to verify a particular
hypothesis. For example, numerous observations may
show that litmus paper placed in an acid, turns red, or that
the same poles of different magnets repel each other.
However, we can never be absolutely sure that this will
occur the *next* time we carry out a similar experiment. To
quote the classic example, the fact of having seen 1,000
white swans does not prove that the next swan seen must be
white. Our knowledge of the world is provisional rather
than absolutely certain. What we can be sure of is what is
not true. Seeing one black swan demonstrates that all swans
are *not* white.

We can sum up the argument in Popper's own words:
'the method of science is the method of bold conjectures
and severe attempts to refute them'.

Is science 'scientific'?

The discussion so far might suggest that there is just one
scientific method, and one basic way in which scientists gain
knowledge. In fact, as we have indicated, there is a difference
between the purely inductive or observational approach (as used
for example in the elaborate system for classifying plants), and
the more deductive scientific method described in Fig. 3.1,
although scientists may employ both in their work. When
compared to this positivistic, rigorous, objective scientific

Fig. 3.4 **Scientific revolutions**

Thomas Kuhn, a historian, has had a considerable impact on the way we think about science. In his book *The Structures of Scientific Revolutions* (University of Chicago Press, 1962), he criticises the commonly accepted view about how science has progressed. This view would suggest that scientists discover elements of truth, and that these are fitted into what is already known. Science, from this point of view, would appear to undergo gradual growth, with the frontiers of what is known being pushed ever further outward. What was previously thought to be true is not rejected, but added to. This is not what has happened, Kuhn says. Scientific work in any field, takes place in the context of the scientists' general viewpoint on the particular thing he or she is studying. For example, until the work of Copernicus, Kepler and later, Galileo, it was believed that the sun went around the earth. This was the **paradigm** or model within which astronomy was studied. The change in perspective on the earth's place in the universe, that occurred after their works had be published, was so complete it has to be called revolutionary, according to Kuhn.

Kuhn emphasises that scientific work does not tend to take place individually. Scientists are part of a community of fellow scientists who see the world in basically the same way. They work within an accepted paradigm which describes 'universally recognised scientific achievements that for a time provide model problems and solutions to a community of practitioners'.

The social sciences, including sociology, Kuhn says, have conflicting models and communities of researchers who are in competition with each other. Sociology is therefore in a 'pre-paradigm state', he argues.

method, with its apparent detachment and precision, sociology would appear to fall a long way short. Sociological knowledge would not seem to be anywhere near as precise or certain.

However this view of science as completely detached and

rational was challenged by Kuhn. He argued persuasively that scientists belonged to distinct scientific communities and tended to let their current conceptions about the nature of the world completely block their ability to see the implications of the contradictory information they themselves were coming up with in their investigations. He maintained that science was not cumulative and did not go through stages of gradual growth, but rather underwent 'revolutionary' changes.

It will be helpful to look at some examples of what Kuhn meant by changes in the way in which scientists conceive of a particular problem and its explanation. A contemporary controversy would relate to the theory of evolution. Most biologists seem to work within one framework of ideas, provided by Darwin in the last century. The ideas of survival of the fittest, and of change coming through natural selection, seem obvious. Only certain Christian fundamentalists would appear to work with a model or 'paradigm' that is completely different, emphasising creation rather than evolution. Yet within this Darwinian paradigm there are actually very important differences between certain scientists, and evidence that contradicts many elements of Darwin's theory has been found. In Kuhn's sense, there are now a number of models or explanations existing side by side but as of yet there is no new overall paradigm available to replace Darwin's theory.

Another example is the change in physics from the mechanistic view of the universe which was outlined particularly by Newton, to the more relativistic modern physics influenced by Einstein's work and the Quantum theory. The extent of this change of paradigm is illustrated by the physicist Capra:

Out of the revolutionary changes that were brought about by modern physics, a consistent world view is now emerging. This view is not shared by the entire physics community, but is being discussed and elaborated by many leading physicists whose interest in their science goes beyond the technical aspects of their research. These scientists are deeply interested in the philosophical implications of modern physics and are trying in an open minded way to improve their understanding of the nature of reality.

In contrast to the mechanistic Cartesian view of the world, the world view emerging from physics can be characterised by words like organic, holistic, and ecological . . . The universe is no longer seen as a machine made up of a multitude of objects, but has to be pictured as one indivisible dynamic whole whose parts are essentially interrelated and can be understood only as patterns of a cosmic process.

Fritjof Capra, *The Turning Point,* Flamingo/Fontana, 1983

An even greater shift may be facing biologists. It is quoted here because it is so very different from the currently accepted view of the world/planet, as passive matter, and therefore challenges our generally accepted paradigm. Jim Lovelock, who has worked with NASA on their space program and has been a Fellow of the Royal Society since 1974, has put forward the hypothesis 'that the earth's living matter – air, ocean and land surfaces – form a complex system which has the capacity to keep our planet a fit place to live' (J.E. Lovelock, *Gaia: a new look at life on earth,* Oxford University Press, 1979). The 'Gaia hypothesis' is not that the earth is conscious as such, but it suggests that the earth is able to self-regulate and act as a living organism. This hypothesis is backed up by Lovelock with impressive evidence. Yet it is doubtful that the presently accepted view of the world will be changed by his work. It is likely just to be ignored.

We have spent some time looking at this question of paradigms, because it is of particular relevance to sociology. Sociology has often been criticised as non-scientific because it has a number of competing types of explanation, or paradigms. This has already been indicated in our earlier discussion of macrosociology and microsociology. The criticism that sociology is unscientific because it has a number of perspectives, like functionalism, marxism and conflict theory, and social action theory, seems less valid when it is recognised that the natural sciences also have competing 'world views' or paradigms. This is a point we will return to in our next section.

One philosopher of science, Feyerabend, maintains that even in their actual methods and experiments scientists are far from 'scientific'. In other words what they *actually* do is very different from what they *say* they do. Science, he says, is a 'sloppy' business. It has no special method. 'For most scientists the slogan "freedom for science" means the freedom to indoctrinate not only those who have joined them but the rest of society as well.' Broad and Wade sum up his ideas in the following way:

Feyerabend not only admits nonrational elements into the scientific process but sees them as dominant. Science, he says, is an ideology, completely shaped at any moment in time by its historical and cultural context. Scientific disputes are resolved not on their merits but by the theatrical and oratorical skills of their advocates, much as are legal cases. There is no one scientific method, good for all times and places; in fact, there is no such thing as scientific method. Despite scientists' claims, the rule in science is that 'anything goes.'

Since there is no one scientific method, success in science depends not only on rational argument but on a mixture of subterfuge, rhetoric, and propaganda, Feyerabend holds. He believes that the distinction commonly made between science and other modes of thought is unjustified, an artificial barrier erected by scientists to set them above their fellow citizens.

W. Broad and N. Wade, Betrayers of Truth,
Simon and Shuster, 1982

While Feyerabend's argument may be a bit extreme it does raise the issue of whether sociology is being unfairly criticised when it is described as unscientific. The actual practice of science, as we saw in our earlier discussion of research into spoonbending, may not be quite as precise as we might have believed.

Our exploration of the relationship between sociology and science would not be complete without consideration of the work of Heisenberg. As we have already seen, a fundamental part of the scientific method involves careful objective measurement and observation. It is assumed that the scientist can observe without influencing the object under observation. We do not expect the weight of an inanimate object, for example, will change just because we weigh it. Heisenberg's *'uncertainty principle'* suggests otherwise. He maintained that the process of observation *always* influenced the object observed to some extent (no matter how small). An example would be taking the pressure of a tyre. The air needed to set the pressure gauge will come from the tyre, and thus the pressure of the tyre after measurement will be slightly less than before. The taking of the pressure has thus changed the pressure. The observer and the observed, according to Heisenberg, are not separate, but part of the same system.

With certain aspects of biological sciences, and with all the social sciences, this uncertainty principle operates all the time. The process of studying individuals or communities changes them in unpredictable ways. Does this mean that sociology cannot possibly be a science? We will assess the position of sociology as a way of 'generating knowledge' in comparison to the natural sciences, in the next section.

Sociology: a science or an art?

When sociology is compared to the method outlined in Fig. 3.1 certain differences are apparent. It is very difficult for sociologists to undertake experiments in the way that natural scientists can, either for the practical reason of the variables being just too complex, or for ethical and moral reasons. Sociological factors like class or power cannot be defined with the precision of concepts like weight or temperature. Even with good definitions it is not possible to measure them with anything like the accuracy that is normal in the natural sciences. However, certain sociologists have assumed that they could emulate the natural sciences, and produce a 'science of society', which was objective and value free. This wish to establish a value free science lies behind the positivist approach to sociology, and particularly the perspective known as *functionalism*.

Positivism and functionalism

From a positivist perspective sociology is a science. It is assumed that society has objective and regular features like those that have been discovered in the natural world. Just as this great system was governed by laws, so it was assumed there were laws that governed society. For many functionalists the purpose of sociology became the discovery of those laws, using approaches and techniques as close to those of the natural sciences as possible. The classic example of this approach is to be found in Durkheim's work, *Suicide*. He tried to establish objectively, that there was a causal relationship between the degree of integration in society and the suicide rate. He was trying to show that sociology could demonstrate that suicide should be explained as a *social* phenomenon, rather than just an individual act.

This positivistic position is closely although by no means exclusively associated with macrosociology. In implementing social surveys, sociologists are generally assuming positivist principles, namely that there are patterns 'out there' in society, to be measured, and that data about them can be collected in an unbiased, value free way.

Radical sociology and conflict theory

By *radical sociology* we are referring to a basically marxist analysis of society. Marx's theory differs very considerably from functionalism in so far as he sees society as composed of groups that are essentially in opposition to each other. Functionalism in contrast tends to stress consensus in society. Yet both approaches share a certain positivistic outlook and assume that there are processes occurring in society that can be measured in an objective way. With radical sociology, the purpose is to show the operations of society objectively, but with concern for the poor, the oppressed and the underprivileged. Marx in particular, as we have already noted, argued that society could be analysed scientifically. Where he completely diverged from functionalism was in his desire not only to analyse society, but to *change* it. The same belief that society can be studied objectively is held by other sociologists who may reject elements of the marxist argument, but still see society as characterised by conflict.

Interpretive sociology

There is another broad perspective in sociology, particularly connected with microsociology. This is called the *social action* or *interpretive approach*. Max Weber (1864–1920) is considered as a principal founder of this perspective. He argued for the need to develop an understanding of how people interpreted the situation that they are in. What did it *mean* to them? The other major contribution to this is G.H. Mead's theory of symbolic interactionism. This concern with meaning introduces a subjective element into sociology, which could not be measured with the same degree of certainty as the aspects of society that positivistic sociologists tended to be concerned with. There is no way that interpretive sociology, with its interest in how people describe and understand their own situation, can be scientific in the classical positivistic sense. Yet Weber stressed the need for value freedom in *measurement*. He maintained that the sociologist's techniques could be objective, even though the sociologists had their own values, and their subject matter was in part, subjective. The issue of values will be explored more fully in Chapter 7.

It is one of the beliefs of the present writer that the strict division of sociology into watertight perspectives is neither very accurate as a description of the discipline, nor very helpful. Yet it must be acknowledged that although sociologists now may borrow ideas and methods from more than one perspective, their sociology often reflects assumptions about society that can be classified under one of the headings just given.

For those who tend to adopt a positivistic framework, the assumption is that sociology can come up with knowledge that is objective, being based on observable social 'facts' and 'laws'. For those who tend towards a more interpretivist position, sociology is seen as providing insight into their world. However, this approach would not claim to be a science in the same way. As we shall see, the method used in interpretive sociology, particularly participant observation, is very different from the classical scientific model.

Sociology is perhaps both a science and an art. It shares certain techniques with science, and when we take the work of Kuhn and Heisenberg into account, we can see that the problem of studying society only differs in terms of degree, rather than in fundamentals, from the natural sciences. Sociology is an art in so far as it provides images of the ever changing nature of society; images that give insight and understanding, even if they lack quantification.

Theory and research strategy

Sociologists, like natural scientists, have a variety of theories, or to use Popper's term, 'conjectures' about the society they study. These theories usually relate to the broad perspectives just mentioned. We need to establish: (a) what is the role of a theory in sociological methodology and (b) what is its relationship to the research process.

The role of theory

Theories provide explanations. They are a collection of *logically linked ideas and generalisations which attempt to demonstrate the reasons behind particular events and processes.* For example, Rosenthal and Jacobson in their book *Pygmalion in the Classroom,* describe and give evidence for the theory of the 'self fulfilling prophecy'. This theory, in brief, explained that the success and failure of students in classrooms was influenced by the expectations of their teachers. The theory thus defined what was relevant for Rosenthal and Jacobson to study. It directed their attention towards certain aspects of behaviour in school, and away from other aspects. It dictated the form of the experiment they undertook. Theory therefore provides the conceptual framework within which research can be carried out. Without a theory, all the natural scientist or sociologist could do is 'just observe'. Lacking a clearly defined problem this would be a futile exercise, because there would be no criteria of what was relevant or irrelevant in the observation. Theories may be very elaborate, as with the Talcott Parsons theory of social systems, or they may be little more than a number of assumptions and generalisations, as with some theories on voting behaviour or theories about aspects of religious activity.

Theory and research

C.W. Mills used the term 'grand theory' to refer to the all embracing theories of writers like Marx and particularly Parsons. Their conceptions were so broad, said Mills, that they attempted to explain the complete operation of society, and assumed that their models of social order were universal. As such they are very difficult, if not impossible, to test. They are dealing with macrosociology. However, they do influence the research process, because they define the guidelines, and define the problems which sociologists then study. Marxists, like Bowles and Gintis, have carried out specific research into education, exploring the role of social class in educational success, because Marx's grand theory suggests this will be relevant.

At the other end of the scale is the concept of 'grounded theory'. This term, used by Glaser and Strauss, refers to theory developed inductively from the situation being researched (see

Reading 8). It is closely associated with microsociology and the social action perspective, with its emphasis on the interpretations of those being studied. Instead of the sociologist starting from a theory based on his or her suppositions, and then going out to test it, the main features of the theory are to be dictated by the definitions and descriptions of the people being studied. Even with this very empirical approach, the sociologist still has to enter the situation with some idea of the problem he or she wishes to study, which gives their research direction and focus.

Between these two extremes comes most sociological research, which is based on what could be called 'middle level theory'. These middle level theories do not attempt to explain the operation of the whole of society. While they may rest on broad assumptions about the nature of society (e.g. a basic consensus or conflict approach), the focus will be on a more limited issue. The work of Goldthorpe and Lockwood on the 'embourgeoisement thesis', Blauner's study of alienation, Lewis on the 'culture of poverty' or Oakley's work on gender, all fall into this category.

The actual methods of research chosen, the techniques that are used, and consequently the type of knowledge or information derived from the research, will vary according to the type of theory that is adopted by the sociologists.

However, we should remember that often sociologists use a variety of research techniques in their work, and may blend aspects of qualitative and quantitative research. We will look next at the quantitative methods of research.

4 Quantitative research: surveys

Any sociological research involves the selection on some basis or other of a group to be studied. The value of the work will in part depend on how those studies can be said to be *representative* of a wider group. Even the account by Jimmy Boyle, mentioned in Chapter 1, is of value sociologically, because it tells us something about gangs in Glasgow and about prisons, that we can assume will bear some sort of relationship to other people's experience. This issue of the *relationship* between the situation researched by the sociologists and the wider society is most important. If there were no broader conclusions that could be drawn from a particular study, no insight into society and social systems, then a book like Boyle's might be of interest but it would have little sociological value.

Sampling is the process whereby people (or information) are selected as being representative of a wider population. The relationship between the sample and the wider population will determine how far the sample can be assumed to be representative of it.

Generally, there can be said to be three levels to the sample. The first we will call the *survey population* or *target population* (see Fig. 4.1). This is the overall population that we are hoping to draw conclusions about, for example it might be recent converts to Christianity or female white-collar workers or housewives or gangs in Glasgow. The survey population may not be people as such, it may be 'households' or 'parish registers' or newspapers or TV news broadcasts. Different books use different titles for this level of the sampling process, including *general universe* (Rose, 1982) and just simply *population*. It should be noted that this survey population is always a sub-group of some larger population (and therefore is itself a type of 'sample').

The second level is commonly called the *sampling frame*. It is from this group that the sample will actually be selected. This might be for instance the telephone directory or the electoral register or a list of employees in a firm or every house in certain

Figure 4.1

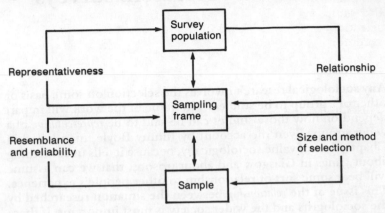

streets of a town. The sampling frame could be identical with the survey population in certain circumstances like a survey of 'all living Nobel prize winners'. The relationship between the sampling frame and the survey population must be known. It must be complete, have no double entries (people occurring twice on the list). The researcher would need to make sure it was up to date and had no 'dead wood' or people who should no longer be on the list.

The third level is the sample itself. This has been defined as 'a small scale representation – a kind of miniature model – of the population from which it is selected' (G. Hoinville *et al.*, 1978). The sample is selected from the sampling frame, using one of a number of techniques.

The representativeness of the sample will depend on two main factors: (a) its size, and (b) the nature and method of its selection. The 'right' size for a sample is not a question of what proportion of the survey population or sampling frame is selected. Rather it depends on the actual number in the sample and the nature of the problem being studied. It is worth noting that polls to determine the voting intentions of the whole population in this country often only interview 1,200 or so respondents. However, this technique has variable success (see Reading 1).

Methods of sampling aim to control bias occurring in the sample itself, distorting the resemblance between the sample and the sampling frame. This is done through various types of selection using an element of chance or randomness. The most common methods are:

Random sampling

This method involves every person (or item) in the sampling frame having an equal chance of being selected. This can be by *systematic sampling* (quasi-random sampling), where for example every fifth or tenth name is chosen from the list. Alternatively, it can be *simple random sampling,* where names are chosen using random number tables or computer produced random numbers (equivalent to, but more accurate than, drawing a specified number out of a hat), to indicate which name to choose.

Stratified sampling

A more representative method than simple random sampling is to specify certain features of the sampling frame that are to be reproduced in the sample. This applies particularly where the population to be sampled is very mixed in terms of relevant characteristics, like race, age, sex, area of residence etc. A random selection can then be made from each sub-set (for example, men and women, West Indians, Asians and white people, those below 40 years of age and those above), so that the final sample faithfully reproduces the proportions of each group that is found in the population as a whole (see Fig. 4.2). Stratified sampling tends to decrease sampling error while cluster sampling tends to increase it.

Cluster or multi-stage sampling

It would be impractical to send researchers all over the country to carry out research, so villages, towns and cities may be chosen to be representative of wider areas. Within a town two or three parts may be selected because they in turn are representative of other areas in the town, and so on.

Figure 4.2 Stratified sampling

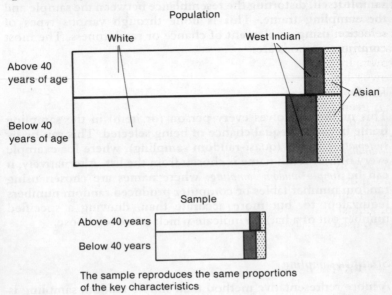

The sample reproduces the same proportions
of the key characteristics

Snowball sampling

When a sample is built up through one respondent (e.g. a member of a religious sect) recommending others who might be prepared to be interviewed, this is a 'snowball' or *opportunity sample*. This technique may be necessary in certain circumstances, but is likely to produce a sample that is far from random.

Quota sampling

Market research often uses quota sampling, when the interviewer in the street will look for fixed numbers of different types of respondent (e.g. black housewives, single men between 20 and 30, houseowners etc.) This method is quick (and cheap). It is not very accurate or as reliable as the more elaborate method of stratified sampling.

Much influential sociological research has been based on quite small samples. Bott, in her well known study of the family,

Family and Social Network (1957), only interviewed twenty families, while Goldthorpe and Lockwood interviewed 229 manual workers for their 'affluent worker' study, and they only came from one town, namely Luton. This had been chosen because it was *atypical*: it was not a traditional working class town but a new town. In other words it may have been typical of certain new towns but deliberately was not representative of more established working class communities. Interpretive sociology often has even smaller samples (indeed, strictly, 'sample' is not really the appropriate word here as the group studied is not representative in the way a normal sample is). Colin Lacey's *Hightown Grammar* (1970) was based on only one school. James Patrick and W.F. Whyte each only worked with one gang. In cases like these we must assess whether such studies can inform us about the larger survey population (families or affluent workers or schools or gangs) especially when classical sampling techniques have not been used.

Asking questions

Much of the skill in all forms of social research revolves around the ability to ask questions. They can range from the specific and succinct found in postal questionnaires and interview schedules like the General Household Survey, to the most unstructured questions, formulated 'on the spot' while involved in participant observation. In each case the aim is similar. It is to acquire information that will be of value to the research project. The method may be different but the sociologist is attempting to further his or her understanding in both cases.

In the next chapter we will return to the less formal context of observation. Here we will look at the specific skills of constructing questionnaires and interview schedules. Before we do this it will be appropriate to consider how all questioning procedures may be assessed. This is done in terms of *validity* and *reliability*.

Validity

The validity of any particular question or research method is determined by whether it *actually measures* what it is supposed to measure. To what extent does it produce answers that are a true reflection of the respondent's belief, experience, or situation? A question like 'How many children do you have?' is likely to produce a valid answer from a mother unless she has a good reason to mislead. However a question like 'What social class do you belong to, upper class, middle class or lower class?' may well be invalid as a measure of class position. It was actually found in the USA that few respondents accepted the label 'lower class' although they were quite happy to call themselves 'working class'. For validity to be high, concepts have to be used in such a way that they do actually measure what they purport to measure. To achieve this is not easy as both theory and method are involved in the process.

The validity of any research method or item can only be assessed by testing the result against some other measure of which one is certain. A watch, for example, can be tested against the Greenwich time signal. The equivalent of a valid check in the social sciences is less easy to come by, as the concepts of 'class position', 'alienation' or 'failure' are necessarily relative and less clear than a 'minute of time'.

Reliability

The reliability of a question or a research procedure is assessed in terms of the *consistency* and *repeatability* of the response. Will the same question asked of the same person in similar circumstances, produce the same answer? For example, the question 'Do you think women should have equal rights to men?' may well produce a consistent response over time. However it may *not* be a valid measure of people's attitude to the gender issue. The response may be conditioned by what the respondent thinks the researcher wants to hear as an answer. Reliability can be checked within a questionnaire by asking the same question in different ways at different points. If a questionnaire is very well constructed it may prove to be completely reliable. However it may not always be valid in its measurements. Often quantitative measures can prove to be reliable but more qualitative measures may have greater validity. A pilot study is a good method of increasing both reliability and validity (see Fig. 4.3).

Fig. 4.3 **Pilot studies**
However skilled the researcher, she or he will not be able to
foresee how people are going to interpret the questions
they are asked or what words or phrases they may find
difficult to understand. An interview schedule or questionnaire should be given a trial run before it is used for the
main survey. This testing exercise is called the pilot study
and can prove invaluable for adjusting the research instru-
ment to make it more reliable and more valid. With a large
survey, the pilot group, which needs to be a small sub
sample of the main sample, can number between thirty and
one hundred. It should, however, cover the full range of
the survey population. If attitude tests are included, that
have to be validated, then the sub-sample may need to be
bigger.

The pilot study can reveal if questions have to be
reworded or the whole questionnaire needs to be reorga-
nised in some way. Rex and Moore piloted their questionnaire into immigrants in the inner city area of Sparkbrook,
in an adjacent area of Birmingham – Balsall Heath –
because it was very similar. Moore wrote 'this gave our first
batch of student interviewers an opportunity to try out
their own skills as well as to test the efficiency of the
scheduled' (R. Moore in Bell and Newby, 1977). They were
therefore not only testing the interview schedule, but also
training their amateur interviewers.

Questionnaire construction

A postal questionnaire will be constructed in a somewhat
different way to an interview schedule but many of the principles
are the same to both. The whole procedure must make sense to
the respondent, it must not confuse, bore or alienate them. The
interview or the questionnaire has to be designed. A plan must
be made setting out what sort of information is required. Then
the plan must be translated into *sequences* of questions that have a
logical pattern to them. One technique used is that of *funnelling*,
where a set of questions starts at a general level (e.g. 'Did you

watch television at all in the last week or two?') and can narrow down to the area the researcher is interested in (e.g. 'Do you think the news coverage of the miners' strike has been fair to the unions?').

Broadly there are two types of questions that can be asked. First, *open-ended* questions leave the respondent free to answer in their own way. A question like 'What do you think about the current situation in Northern Ireland?' allows the person asked to formulate their answer as they wish. 'Tell me your main impressions of your schooldays' is much more open than 'Did you find school boring? Second, *closed* questions, tend to completely limit the reply to a 'yes/no' choice or a fixed set of responses. For factual questions like 'Were you born in Great Britain?', this is an advantage. Various answers may be offered in the question, e.g. 'Would you say, on the whole that your doctor is **a** very helpful, **b** helpful, **c** unhelpful, **d** very unhelpful, **e** don't know?'. A closed question like this is much easier to code (see Fig. 4.2) and the results can be easily computed. The open-ended questions may increase insight but it will be more difficult to compare data from different respondents and to treat the data statistically.

Where possible questions should be kept short and unambiguous. The clearer and more specific the questions are, the more reliable the response is likely to be. The phrasing of questions is quite an art and questions have to be scrutinised carefully to make sure they are precise and clear. 'How long have you lived here?' is much too vague if what you want to know is 'How long have you lived in your current house or flat?'. 'Here' in the previous question could mean 'house' or 'town' or even 'country'. Even when questions are clear they must be carefully assessed to eliminate emotional language, leading questions and bias. Consider the following unsubtle examples:

'Do you think people should be allowed to scrounge on social security?'
'With the Russian threat do we have any choice but to keep nuclear weapons?'
'Research has shown that men are less tolerant than women on the whole. Do you believe this is true?'
'Do you think the labour movement is now too radical and has become a threat to democracy?'

Fig. 4.4 Coding

Information from interviews and questionnaires is often analysed statistically. To make this task easier, closed questions are usually coded on the interview schedule itself, so that the interviewer only has to ring the number equivalent to the answer given. For example:

Q. How many children do
   you have?

		circle one
	none	1
	one	2
	two	3
	three	4
	four or more	5

In a questionnaire filled in by the respondents themselves, the coding may be done by them:

Q. Will you definitely vote in
   the next general election?

		tick one box
	yes	1
	no	2
	don't know	3

When the interview schedules or questionnaires are gathered in, precoded information can be quickly transferred onto cards or 'punched' in to a computer. With open-ended questions, coding if applicable, will be done after the questionnaires are all completed, using a 'coding frame' which will be based on answers recorded in the first hundred responses or so. The responses actually given in this first batch will determine the categories of the coding frame.

Words like 'scrounge' are emotional and invite a negative response. The phrase 'Russian threat' will tend to lead the respondent to a particular answer, while the opening 'Research has shown' in a question, may include what is called prestige-bias, where the respondent feels pressured to agree. The final example is of a 'double question' where there may be agreement with one part (e.g. 'too radical') but disagreement with the other (e.g. 'threat to democracy').

Other problems that may occur are those where the memory of the respondent is taxed or where sensitive issues have to be dealt with. Where the individual may not remember it is important that there is no pressure causing them to make up an answer. With sensitive issues like sex, family relationships, race, politics etc. the questions have to be very skilfully worded and introduced with great care. It is usually not possible to tackle complex issues like this in a postal questionnaire.

Attitude measurement

The problem of measuring attitudes is a difficult one. In essence the methods involve the construction of a *scale* against which the attitude towards a particular idea can be measured. In one technique a series of statements can be listed and the respondent has to tick where their reply would be. For example:

	strongly agree	agree	uncertain	disagree	strongly disagree
It is not easy to keep one's temper with young children.					

Establishing the validity of attitude measurements is not easy. There is always the problem for researchers of the gap between the answer given to an attitude question – an answer that may be genuinely believed – and the actual behaviour of the person in question.

Postal questionnaires

The postal questionnaire can be a fairly cheap method of covering a large sample. It has been estimated that it costs about a third of an equivalent interview survey. It is especially useful when coverage of a wide geographical area is important. Another advantage it has is it gives individuals time to think about their answers and to look up information. They do not feel as much under pressure as they might with an interviewer present. The questionnaire has to be designed with great skill, to be attractive and interesting to answer as it has to overcome the reluctance which most people feel to giving up their time. The great problem with a postal questionnaire is the low response rate which can be as little as 40 to 60 per cent. This can be improved by using a tactful covering letter and then following this up with a couple of reminders about 10 days and 20 days after the initial mailing. Even so the response rate seldom exceeds 80 per cent. However, research indicates that with response rates of 70 per cent or above, the non-responses tend to be randomly distributed.

Postal surveys can be used as forerunner to interviews. The whole sample may be subsequently interviewed or a specific sub-sample chosen for a more in-depth study.

Interviews

Interviews require social skills on the part of the interviewer. A well designed interview schedule still has to be effectively administered. The interviewer has to establish *rapport* with the respondents. This means they must be accepted and gain the agreement of the respondent to conduct the interview. The advantages of the interview are that they can go into greater detail and also move into more sensitive and complex domains than questionnaires. Questions can be explained and answers can be probed to find out what the interviewee really means.

There is of course always the risk that the interviewers themselves may introduce bias by seeming to favour certain answers over others. A black interviewer may receive different answers to a white interviewer. A woman may be able to interview other women more effectively than a man (see Oakley's account, Reading 14).

Interviews can vary greatly from the very formal and structured to the informal and open ended. With the latter the edge between interviewing and participant observation may well become blurred. We will turn to a consideration of participant observation in the following chapter.

5 Qualitative research: observation

The field study tradition

Participant observation and the field study tradition has its roots firmly in the anthropological tradition of researchers like Malinowski, Margaret Mead and Evans–Pritchard. The richly fascinating and influential descriptions which they brought back of 'primitive' peoples demonstrated the value of observation for the studying of strange and exotic cultures. The accuracy of observations have sometimes been called into dispute (see Reading 12) but the techniques developed by anthropologists have also been used in sociology. The other root of participant observation is to be found particularly in the work of George Herbert Mead. His work on the 'social self' and the theory of symbolic interactionism, stressed the need to take account of the way individuals communicated, and the meanings these communications had for the participants.

Ackroyd and Hughes argue that an interpretive perspective requires different methods to those of quantitative sociology. They explain the participant observation approach this way:

> It is a view which rejects the quantitative stance of much social science research in favour of one which stresses instead a more qualitative approach. The argument rests very much on the contention that social life is constructed in and through meanings which cannot be studied in terms of deterministic laws, but must be understood interpretively; a process made possible only by some form of participation in, and experience of, that which is to be understood.

> We have made the point that the method of participant observation is closely associated with a particular theoretical perspective in sociology; a perspective which stresses the interactive and negotiated character of the social order, created in and through the meanings actors use to make sense of and interpret the world in which they live. There is little sense

here of an objective social structure of the kind presupposed by the early social surveyors. Instead the social structure is seen as a multitude of scenic processes, constantly moving and changing as actors negotiate and renegotaite their course of action. There is little conception too of society as a macro-structure, and a preference for studying rather limited sections of visible social life: those groups and processes tangible and familiar to the actors concerned.

Such small scale worlds, plus the injunction that the social investigator should examine them from the point of view of the participants themselves, provide the putative participant observer with the first of his, or her, problems; gaining access or entry. This is often a matter of fine judgement. One of the major arguments for participant observation is that it allows the study of persons and groups in their natural habitat as opposed to the artificial circumstances of the laboratory or the detached and often remote method of the survey interview.

S. Ackroyd and J.A. Hughes, *Data Collection in Context,*
Longman, 1981

The basis of participant observation has been described as anti-positivism. Certainly the theory that it rests on is very different to positivism and macrosociology. This is reflected in the methods adopted in participant observation.

Methods of participant observation

Evans-Pritchard describes how he tried to learn how to conduct field research:

When I was a serious young student in London I thought I should get a few tips from experienced field workers before setting out for central Africa. I first sought advice from Westermarck. All I got from him was 'don't converse with an informant for more than twenty minutes because if you aren't bored by that time he will be.' Very good advice, even if somewhat inadequate. I sought instruction from Haddon, a man foremost in field-research. He told me that it was really all quite simple; one should always behave as a gentleman. Also very good advice. My teacher Seligman told me to take ten grains of quinine every night and to keep off women. The famous Egyptologist, Sir Flinders Petrie, just told me not to bother about drinking dirty water as one soon became immune to it. Finally, I asked Malinowski and was told not to be a bloody fool.

Evans-Pritchard, quoted in Burgess, 1982

A model of participant observation

Participant observation, as the name suggests, involves the researcher becoming part of a community in order to study that community. When Erving Goffman wanted to study a mental institution he took a job as a hospital orderly and in that role, observed the day to day interactions in the hospital, which he wrote about in his book *Asylums* (1968). He was, in a sense, a researcher 'in disguise'. Leon Festinger (1956) joined a religious sect and passed as a sect member, in order to observe them. Laud Humphreys, (1970) study of homosexuals necessitated adopting the role of 'deviant' (see Fig 5.1) at certain points of time. Gold (1958) has described the roles each of these researchers were adopting as 'complete participant'. He suggest three other roles which the researcher can adopt: the 'participant-as-observer', the 'observer-as-participant' and the 'complete observer'.

The latter role of complete observer is almost impossible to fulfill, for the very presence of the observer is a type of participation. R. King attempted this in his research into infants' school classrooms (*All Things Bright and Beautiful,* 1978). By not getting involved in conversation he aimed to 'effectively disappear'. The observer-as-participant is really only applicable, according to God, if only one interview is carried out on one occasion. So in effect participant observation generally involves the first two categories.

There is a definite problem to be faced with complete observation and that is 'going native'. Some anthropologists have ceased to research and just joined the communities that they were studying. A researcher who has had to 'adopt native costume' in order to pass himself or herself off as a member of the community, may come to identify so closely with that community that he or she loses all objectivity. However, there is a risk involved in trying to maintain objectivity (through taking notes, leaving the situation regularly, not becoming too involved) and that is that the researcher may be exposed. The

Fig. 5.1 **Tearoom trade**

The 'tearooms' that Laud Humphreys spent many hours in during his research, were not cafeterias in American parks but public conveniences for men. His research was into the 'secret deviants' who used the cover of these toilets for their furtive and casual sexual encounters. They were 'secret' in the sense that often they were married men and were by no means necessarily members of the gay community. In the dialect of this community, they were the 'closet queens'.

As they ran the serious risk of imprisonment if caught and as the potential sexual partners were often completely unknown to each other, the way in which intentions were communicated and approaches made in the public ano-nimity of the 'tearooms', was an interesting sociological problem. Humphreys could only effectively study it by observation. Few would have been prepared to allow him to interview them. Mostly Humphreys had to hide his researcher's role, and adopt the tearoom role of a 'watcher'. He would keep a lookout, while others engaged in sex. As this role was necessary and combined with the accepted role – in tearooms – of 'voyeur', he was able to successfully complete this stage of his research. As a result of his observations, he succeeded in mapping out the usual pattern of these unusual encounters.

Humphreys, once accepted as part of the scene, was able to engage twelve participants in conversation and revealed his research interests to them. All were happy to talk, provided their complete anonymity was preserved. How-ever as a sample they could not be considered as repre-sentative. As Humphreys admits, 'Their willingness to cooperate sets them apart from those they are meant to represent'. As we shall see, getting a proper sample took many months of hard and patient work.

'disguise' may be penetrated. The role clearly is not an easy one.

For this reason many observers have followed the observer-as-participant role. The observer joins a community but it is known that they are doing research. Whyte, in his work in an American slum, used this strategy saying he was researching in order to write a book (see Fig 5.2). C. Lacey (*Hightown Grammar,* 1970) taught at a Manchester grammar school while doing his research there. He was able to interview and use questionnaires to back up his observations because his researcher status was accepted.

Collins and Pinch, whose work as scientists investigating spoon-bending we have considered already, have suggested an alternative 'ideal type' model of participant observation. They argue that the two ends of Gold's scale, complete participation and complete observation, orginate from quite different methodological and theoretical positions (interpretivism and positivism). A better scale, they suggest, would be between 'unobtrusive measures', which would include the work of people like Festinger and Humphries, and 'participant comprehension', which was the method they used. They maintain that:

> Comprehension will have been achieved when what once seemed irritating and incoherent comes to follow naturally. The investigator has no responsibility to 'keep it all straight' nor to be able to reproduce the details of all the interactions that are observed. On the contrary, the investigator *him/herself* should come to be able to act in the same way as native members 'as a matter of course' rather than remember or record the details of *their* interactions.
>
> H.M. Collins 1984 *op. cit.*

Later they use the phrase 'participant introspection', which suggests that the result of this method is that the researcher has so internalised the 'native role', that by thinking about their own experiences they are able to gain the necessary insights.

As will be appreciated, participant observation, particularly in its more extreme participant comprehension method, raises all sorts of issues relating to objectivity. It also raises certain ethical issues. Participant comprehension and complete participation, in the sense that we have already used these terms, are *covert* methods of study. The researchers do not reveal that they are carrying out research. In the more *overt* methods of participant-as-observer etc. the group or community are at least more aware that they are being observed, and may have some choice in the matter. Both these issues will be explored in more detail later.

Sampling

All social research involves some kind of sample and participant observation is no exception. The community that is observed,the gang that is joined, the sect that is infiltrated, all have to be selected on some criterion or other. The 'tearooms' that Humphries chose to look at were not a random cross-section but were meant to be representative of those that were 'active', in the sense that they were used by homosexuals. In this, and similar research, the purpose is to be able to come up with conclusions of general significance that go beyond the specific groups studies. The relationship between the sample and the wider population needs to be considered. John Honigmann affirms that 'an ethnographer cannot avoid selecting some people, objects or events for study, thereby removing, for a time at least, the possibility of studying others'. As this is the case, he gives a warning: 'However strongly some stimuli "compel" the ethnographer's attention, it will pay him to be aware of the character of his sample . . .' (J. Honigmann, Burgess 1982); in other words the researcher must not let the glamorous or the unusual distort his sampling procedures and introduce bias.

Entry, gatekeepers and key informants

The hopeful researcher is often faced with the considerable difficulty of gaining an entry to the group they wish to study. We have already seen that if covert research is to be undertaken then a 'native costume' must be acquired. In other words the researcher has to pass for one of the group they are interested in or achieve an acceptable 'outsider' role. Humphries managed this by his casual dress and 'correct behaviour' in the tearooms. Gans points out the limitation for a covert role if the observer is studying a whole community, as necessarily they can only join certain groups and are excluded from others. Entry may not be equally easy to different parts of the community:

> I have always told people right from the start that I was a
> researcher, and hoped that they would accept me as such. In
> Levittown this created no problem; I explained I was studying
> how a group of strangers makes a community, and this was a
> nicely impersonal subject in which the Levittowners, then still

strangers to one another, were also intensely interested. In the West End, entry was more difficult, for working class people are less familiar with research and more suspicious of middle class intruders of any kind. They will not talk easily with an outsider or let him into their groups, which, being based largely on kinship, have little room for visiting strangers. Eventually, however, they do permit entry to the researcher, provided they see him often enough to establish trust in him, and have no reason to doubt the purpose of his research.

H. Gans, in *Institutions and the Person,* ed. H. Hecker *et al,* 1968

Access to groups may be controlled by specific people. These could be sect leaders, office managers, prison governors, union officials and the like. They can be called 'gatekeepers'. A research setting, like a school, may have various gatekeepers, including the headmaster and specific class teachers. Even influential students or pupils may determine access to certain groups of children.

For Whyte's study, the crucial element was Doc, a young gang leader who was prepared to help him with his research, and acted as a 'gatekeeper'. 'As long as I was with Doc and vouched for by him no one asked me who I was or what I was doing.' Doc enabled Whyte to gain access to many of the people and groups that he wanted to study. Doc also proved to be a key informant providing important information about the neighbourhood in general (see Fig. 5.2).

Adopting a role

Even after the participant observer has managed to enter a group, he (or she) can still be under considerable pressure. He has to establish a role for himself, in the community or groups he has joined, while maintaining a balance between observing and participating. For Gans, 'participant observation requires the suppression or postponement of satisfying personal needs and it also means pretending to feelings about the participation itself that may not be real. The fieldworker is thus in some ways like a politician; he participates with a hidden agenda and cannot talk freely about himself.'

Valdo Pons had the added disadvantage (or advantage?) in his research into local community life in an African town in the

Fig. 5.2 Street corner society
Much Chicago based research in the 1930s was concerned
with the idea of social disorganisation in slum areas. W.F.
Whyte's study of Cornerville, an Italian American down-
town area, demonstrated that life was much more structured and organised than expected. Whyte used the 'cover'
that he was writing a book about Cornerville, to explain his
presence. However, he found that 'acceptance in the dis-
trict depended on the personal relationships I developed
far more than any explanations I might give'. He was
fortunate that Doc, the leader of the Norton Street gang,
accepted him and acted as a key informant. Doc was to play
a crucial part in the research.

> This full awareness of the nature of my study stimulated
> Doc to look for and point out to me the sorts of
> observations that I was interested in. Often when I
> picked him up at the flat where he lived with his sister
> and brother-in-law, he said to me: 'Bill, you should have
> been around last night. You would have been interested
> in this.' And then he would go to tell me what had
> happened. Such accounts were always interesting and
> relevant to my study. Doc found this experience of
> working with me interesting and enjoyable, and yet the
> relationship had its drawbacks. He once commented:
> 'You've slowed me up plenty since you've been down
> here. Now, when I do something, I have to think what
> Bill Whyte will want to know about it and how I can
> explain it. Before I used to do things by instinct.'
> However, Doc did not seem to see this as a serious
> handicap. Actually, without any training he was such a
> perceptive observer that it only needed a little stimulus
> to help him to make explicit much of the dynamics of
> the social organisation of Cornerville.
>
> W.F. Whyte, *Street Corner Society*,
> University of Chicago Press, 1955

Congo, that he was a white European. 'I was conspicuous and out of place in the area, and I had no pre-existing links there . . . I was an outsider, but so were many of the inhabitants.' He found he was able to enter some social situation as easily as the locals. As he was able to do tasks for people, like writing letters and explaining the procedures for registering at the labour exchange, he could use his very European status to make some contacts. 'I found that I came to know and identify people more rapidly than many a newcomer, and the information which I accumulated over the course of a few months enabled me in some cases to follow conversations about local people better than some of the residents themselves.' (V. Pons, *Stanleyville*, 1969).

Richard Jenkins had the problem of adopting a suitable role in order to undertake an observational study in Belfast. He was helped by the fact that he was able, more or less legitimately, to pass himself off as a youth worker, a role local people understood and could relate to (see Fig. 5.3). Such a role gave him good access to most groups he was interested in but ironically he found interviewing the 'respectable' girls ('Citizens' as he calls them) quite difficult, as they tended to avoid any associations with youth workers.

Field work for a female observer can have added difficulties. Whether the research is overt or covert there can always be the problem of 'hustling' or unwanted male attentions. 'Particularly in the male dominated settings, where the observer is talking to one male at a time, the male–female games come early to the fore.' (Lois Easterday *et al.*, in Burgess, 1982). The female researcher, according to Easterday and her colleagues, is often treated as an errand girl or 'go-fer' when doing observation. Other imposed roles are 'mascot' and 'surrogate daughter'. However being female can have its advantages too.

> The previously mentioned problem of not being taken seriously can work to one's benefit. If a researcher is not taken seriously because she is a young female, this can facilitate entrée into an otherwise difficult or inaccessible setting. In one instance one of us was granted access to a school of mortuary science to which an older, well known female researcher had been denied access. The young researcher was taken in on a 'mascot' basis by one of the male faculty members. The researcher's position and work were fully

Fig. 5.3 Lads, citizens and ordinary kids
With all the violence and intimidation in Belfast which started more than a decade ago, it is a far from easy place to study. Richard Jenkins described the aim of his research as:

> an attempt to document and understand the passage between adolescence and adulthood, between education and the labour market, of the young men and women of a housing estate on the outskirts of Belfast. As such it addresses itself to two kinds of debate: youth culture and the transition from school on the one hand, and the Northern Ireland situation on the other.
>
> R. Jenkins, *Lads, Citizens and Ordinary Kids,*
> Routledge and Kegan Paul, 1983

The problem for the researcher here is that outsiders are looked upon with considerable distrust. Jenkins was faced with the problem of what 'role' to adopt. Generally people in 'Ballyhightown' did not understand the role of 'researcher' or 'student' and so it was easier for him to assume the role of youth worker. He had the advantage that in the year prior to his research he had been employed as a youth worker, and now helped on a voluntary basis.

He describeds himself as an anthropologist and sees his work as ethnography or the observation of people in their natural setting. His research suggested three categories of youth in Ballyhightown: the 'Lads' (all male), the 'Citizens' (female), and the 'Ordinary Kids' (both male and female). These categories arose, he said, from the findings of the research itself, rather than being imposed by prior theory, and formed the basis of the samples that he chose to interview subsequently.

described to the 'gatekeeper', the dean of the school. In a rather offhand way – 'Oh sure, come on in' – he granted the access. His only concern was that the researcher always dress appropriately for the setting.

Easterday *et al., op. cit.*

'Talking': the problem of interviewing

While much participant observation work just involves the skills of careful observation, questioning and interviews can also be vital. If researchers are going to really see the world through the eyes of the group they are studying, then they must be able to use the technique of the *unstructured interview*. This, as its name suggests, is a skilful conversation where the researcher guides, prompts and probes his or her 'witness' in order to gain information. While unstructured it should not be unprepared. The researcher would be wasting their own time if they lacked the specialised knowledge of their informants (whether union officials, gang leaders, school inspectors or whoever else they are studying) to such an extent that they did not know the *right* questions to ask. Yet often these interviews will also be *non-directive*. They will permit the witness/informant to take the discussion in the direction which they see as relevant, enabling the researcher to come to understand their interpretation and view of the world.

As with all interviews there is the problem of verifying what has been said, even if the researcher has adopted a covert role. A greater problem is accurately recording what has been said and considerable concentration and memorative powers must be exercised by the researcher, combined with finding the first opportunity to make notes.

It would be wrong to conclude that participant observation never involves formal interviews. Generally sociologists choose a range of techniques in their studies. They will often use a variety of methods to 'triangulate' on their research problem. These research strategies may reflect their theoretical outlook, but often the actual methods used are quite broad. Humphreys employed complex and elaborate means to establish a sample of homosexual men, whom he was able to follow up a year after completing his observations. He carried out formal interviews into their socio-economic background. (He had been able to combine this sample into another unrelated piece of research and asked no questions at all to indicate that he knew of their homosexuality.) In other words he used quantitative techniques to establish the background for his unique qualitative data.

When in the field the overt observer in particular faces considerable difficulties in recording his or her data. If it is not done quickly the material will almost certainly be partly forgotten or lost.

Recording data

During participant observation, keeping the field diary becomes a prime focus of the day. The advice so often given is 'write-everything-down-you-never-know-what-might-be-important-later', as Jenkins remarks. The very good reason for this is that as the researcher comes to *participate* more, so he or she ceases to notice the commonplace. If it is not recorded while it is still strange, it may be overlooked later.

Whyte explains in his appendix to *Street Corner Society*, that he first put all his notes in chronological order in a single folder. As time passed and material grew, this ceased to be adequate.

> Without really thinking the problem through, I began filing the material [by groups], reasoning that I could redivide it on a topic basis when I had better knowledge of what the relevant topics should be. As the material in the folders piled up, I began to realise that the organisation of notes by social groups fitted in with the way my study was developing.
>
> Whyte, 1955

After some time the material in each of the folders became so considerable that he had to develop an index for each one.

Field notes may range from jottings to theoretical analysis. Burgess (1982) suggests that full field notes will be of three basic kinds: substantive field notes, giving details of major observations and conversations, methodological field notes, consisting mainly of details about the circumstances of collecting data and the techniques used, and analytical field notes, in which hypotheses are developed and theories explored.

It goes without saying that precision, clarity, detail and accuracy are of the upmost importance during this stage. This forms the empirical foundation of any subsequent theorising.

Ethical issues

Participant observation has been criticised as unethical as it often involves subterfuge and deceit. It can also lead researchers into difficulties. Powdermaker, while researching in the Southern United States, found herself caught up with a lynch mob. She did not know what to do. She concluded that to go to the police would not have helped and would have ruined her research, as would trying to persuade the mob to behave otherwise. She was greatly relieved when the man being hunted, escaped. Not so lucky was Hunter Thompson who was beaten up by Hell's Angels when he refused to pay them money for the 'privilege' of having 'hung around' observing them (Burgess, 1982).

Covert or disguised participant observation courts these sort of problems and dilemmas. Some question the right of the researchers, whatever their motives, to impose themselves on the unsuspecting, who have no choice over the matter. 'Friend-ship can become transformed into capital, personal revelation into data, and conflict into illumination,' argues Rock (quoted in Ackroyd and Hughes, 1981).

Humphreys defends his work and similar studies, on the ground that the knowledge is important, because others, parti-cularly the media and the courts, can make assumptions that are not in any way informed by research, but very greatly influence policy and action. He points out what happened when this knowledge is lacking, quoting from a police report, which rested on an assumption that young people were in danger from homosexual abuse (something contradicted by *all* of Humphreys subsequent research).

> In one toilet, which had no partitions between johns, we caught a guy sitting on one john reaching over for the genitals of a boy sitting on another. It wasn't very nice work believe me.

Humphreys comments on the effects ill-informed reports like this had:

> This may not have been 'very nice work' for the investigator quoted; however, the crackdown on homosexuals in Boise, Idaho, of which his work was a part, produced results. Before the scandal ended in 1956, more than 1,400 persons were questioned and twenty arrested; a city of 50,000 was caught up in panic; one of the boys involved murdered his father; the chief of police was fired, as was the local probation officer; and the son of a city councilman was discharged from West

Point. Most tragic of all, nine men were convicted of homosexual offences and sentenced to the state penitentiary, their sentences ranging from five years to life, and some of these men left families behind them.

Humphreys, 1970

There is no easy solution to the ethical dilemma of what is a legitimate subject for study and what is a legitimate method. Humphreys insists that the anonymity and protection of his subjects was his primary interest. Certainly this is an issue that does not just affect participant observation but rather confronts all social research to a greater or lesser extent.

Oral histories

Books and accounts that derive from participant observation are often profusely illustrated with extracts from the conversations with those being studied. The richness and immediacy of these materials serve to provide a window on the world that is being observed. By quoting in detail the words of 'witnesses', the reader is given access to the meanings and interpretations of the community being studied, or so it is hoped. In some cases the extracts will be organised according to certain theoretical considerations, as in Paul Willis's *Learning to Labour*.

Other researchers present their argument virtually entirely in the words of those they are interested in. Seabrook's study of a working class childhood is a case in point (see Reading 10). It could be maintained that this method lets the data speak for itself; the reader is given the material unadulterated, and can make his own judgement. However even such oral testimonies have to be selected, edited and arranged, and their accuracy has to be assessed. We will look at the implications of using oral and documentary material in the next chapter.

6 Evaluating sociological research

The research process

Sociological research is a complex enterprise involving a dynamic interplay between personal values, theories and practical data gathering skills. Different sociologists, looking at the same community but not starting from the same theoretical viewpoint, may direct their attention to different aspects of the place they are studying and come up with a strongly contrasting results. A well known example of this is the study of the Mexican village of Tepoztlan by Robert Redfield (*The Folk Society*, 1947) in the 1930s and later by Oscar Lewis (*Life in a Mexican Village*, 1949). To read their accounts it would appear as though they had been looking at totally different villages (see Fig. 6.1).

What is apparent is that their starting point in terms of theory and values, and the sort of research that this led them to undertake, was very different. This does not necessarily mean that one was 'right' and the other 'wrong'. It does however highlight the need to be able to assess the effectiveness of particular methodologies in sociology and see them in their overall context. We must, to use Gerry Rose's phrase, be able to 'decipher sociological research'. To do this, we will use a model of the research process. It is, in itself, something of an 'ideal type' (see Chapter 7) and we are not arguing that all research follows this pattern. Nevertheless we can say that most research contains the following elements: theory, hypothesis, operationalism, field work and results. The process of research can be summed up in diagramatic form (see Fig. 6.2). This diagram clearly is similar to the model given earlier of the scientific method (see Fig. 3.1, page 18). The model as set out here applies particularly to quantitative research methods. An approach to evaluating qualitative research is given later in this chapter.

It must be emphasised that what sociologists *actually do* may diverge quite sharply from this model. However as Rose (1982) points out, the research is subsequently written up in a format

Fig. 6.1 **Studies of Tepotzlan**
What is found in sociological research may be profoundly
affected by the orientation and interest of the researcher.
Two studies of the same Mexican village, separated by
about ten years, came to very different conclusions. Newby
and Lee describe the contrasting findings:

> Whereas Redfield had discovered a homogenious,
> smoothly functioning, well integrated, contented, stable
> and harmonious community, Lewis, somewhat unner-
> vingly, emphasised 'the underlying individualism of
> Tepotzlan institutions and character, the lack of coop-
> eration, the tensions between villages within the *munici-*
> *pio,* the schisms within the village, the pervading quality
> of fear, envy and distrust, in interpersonal relations'
> (Lewis, *op.cit.*). The discrepancies between the two
> accounts are very marked and cannot be accounted for
> by changes in Tepotzlan during the intervening period,
> nor by Lewis's advantages of working with more personn-
> nel and resources and possessing the benefit of hind-
> sight. Rather the differences are due to the fact that
> Redfield and Lewis were operating with different
> theoretical orientations which influenced the selection
> and coverage of the data and the way in which the data
> were organised. For Redfield the folk-urban continuum
> formed the organising principle of his ethnographic
> account. Consequently the emphasis throughout his
> study is on cooperative and unifying factors. He glosses
> over evidence of violence, cruelty, disease, suffering,
> poverty, economic and social maladjustment and poli-
> tical schisms.
>
> D. Lee and H. Newby, *The Problem of Sociology,*
> Hutchinson, 1983

like this. As we would expect, the 'path' of the research,
particularly the starting point, may differ substantially between
those involved in macrosociology and those doing microso-
ciollogy. The former will tend to work (or claim to work)
deductively from theory to field work and back to theory. The

Figure 6.2 The research process (adapted from G. Rose, 1982)

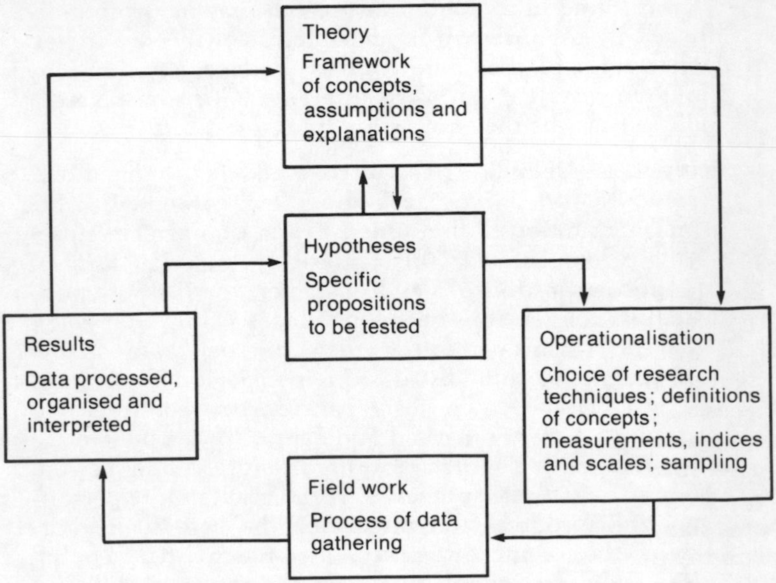

latter will often develop a more grounded theory, which will evolve from their field work. In each case the different key elements of the research process can be analysed. We will look more closely at these next.

The elements of the research process

Theory

Under this heading we are including the general *theoretical assumptions* which underlie the research, whether functionalist, marxist, conflict, social action or some branch or combination of these. This overall theoretical framework will include certain *principal concepts*, which will need to be recognised. The *purpose* of the research and the *value orientations* of the researcher can be considered to influence this level as well. Finally, the way in which *explanations* of social reality are formulated will be included.

Hypotheses

These are *specific propositions to be tested*. In a piece of research there may be one main hypothesis or many. They may not be explicitly spelt out.

Operationalism

This is a pivotal element of research. In its broadest sense it involves the selection of the overall *research strategy* and specific field work techniques, which will be strongly influenced by theoretical orientations. The *sample* that is going to be studied needs to be chosen. The method of choice of the sample will determine how far the results of the research can be generalised to a broader population (see Chapter 4). It is also at this stage that the *concepts* implicit in the theory are organised and formulated in such a way as to be made *measurable*. The concepts have to be expressed in terms that allow some quantification and enable data about them to be collected. This will involve the development of *indices* and *scales* relating the concepts under consideration. It will also include problems of questionnaire design.

Field work

This refers to the actual process of *gathering data*. It may be by methods as diverse as documentary research or observation, experimentation or social surveys. The variety of methods used have been discussed in the previous two chapters.

Results

Data, once gathered, has to be *organised and interpreted*. This may involve, for example, sophisticated statistical techniques and computation or the analysis of hours of transcribed interview material. The data when processed can then be assessed in relationship to the general theory or specific hypotheses.

An example: 'White-Collar Work'

A recent piece of research of a mainly quantitative nature will provide an example of the evaluation of the research process. *White-Collar Work,* by K. Prandy, A. Stewart and R. Blackburn (1982) is a study of non-manual workers ranging from clerks and production supervisors to professionals and top managers. Space will not permit a detailed summary of the book or even the research techniques used. However the authors clearly state their research procedure, which makes the 'deciphering' process easier. The research is part of a general concern with studies of work and trade unionism, although in this book the authors say their focus is on the way work is experienced. The main variables being considered are to do with rewards: income, status, security, social interaction and promotion. This theme of what people expect to get out of work is, in part, a development of Goldthorpe and Lockwood's study *The Affluent Worker* (1968), with its emphasis on orientations to work. No equivalent study had been made of the orientations of non-manual workers, until this research.

We will analyse their research in terms of the various stages already outlined.

Theory

The important point that needs to be made here is that Prandy *et al.* do not appear to fit into any specific theoretical niche. While their research overall is quantitative, they are not 'functionalists', 'marxists' or 'social interactionists'. Like much current sociology, their theory contains elements of a conflict approach. They also recognise the need to take individual perceptions and expectations into account in the tradition of social action theory, while drawing on concepts common to many industrial studies. Their concern they say is 'with the variations in the way work is experienced and the different forms of adaptations and outcomes'. The white-collar worker is in an unequal class system. The workers' reaction to this is in accord with how they see their own situation, which Prandy *et al.* argue ties in with the limits of their previous experience. They summarise their approach to the question of expectations of rewards as follows:

We decided firstly to concentrate our attention on five types of rewards that are sought, at least by a significant number of workers, in the employment situation. For purposes of analysis, they are presented under the broad headings of income, security, status, social relationships and intrinsic job rewards. However, we are aware of elements of diversity within their composition – the last, for example, includes such matters as control, variety and use of abilities.

Secondly, we would anticipate that there are several characteristics of individuals, relating to their social background and experience that would influence the nature of their orientations towards work . . . orientations involve both the importance of the various rewards, primarily the five listed above, and their expected levels.

Prandy *et al., op. cit.*

The relative position of the workers with regard to the reward structure was considered an important 'frame of reference'.

Hypotheses

In the early part of the book specific hypotheses are stated. These are precise enough to be tested (and refuted). Two examples are given here of the sort of hypotheses they are working with:

'continued experience of a level of rewards below that expected is likely to lead to a downward revision of expectations.' (Prandy *et al*. p.7)

'At a basic level we postulate that individuals whose level of rewards do not match up to their expectations, will either seek to avoid it or themselves in such a way so as to reduce the discrepancy.' (Prandy *et al*. p.74)

These and other hypotheses could be tested statistically, in the study, because the data produced by the research could be converted into numerical form.

Operationalism

We have suggested that this is the stage in the research process at which the strategy for the fieldwork is decided, and the specific groups that are going to be studied are selected. With a research project like *White-Collar Work*, which takes a quantitative approach, the size of the sample and its selection become of considerable importance. Much attention is given in the book to this aspect. We learn that they decided to limit the research to within a 60 mile radius of Cambridge (the authors are all Cambridge based). While they claim that 'it includes areas of

---

Fig 6.3 Questions and scales
The first four questions are taken from the interview schedule used in *White-Collar Work*. This schedule would be used by the interviewers, and the questions read to the respondents. The final sentence in italics is a note to the interviewer.

Considering a normal working day for you, for example yesterday (or last working day):

28. (a) How many of your superiors did you see to talk to?
    (b) How long altogether did this take?
29. (a) How many of your subordinates did you see to talk to?
    (b) How long altogether did this take?
30. (a) How many other people did you see to talk to?
    (b) How long altogether did this take?
31. You have already given us information on several aspects of your job. No-one has a perfect job, and almost everyone could think of ways in which his job could be improved. Some improvements would obviously be more important than others. On these cards are various aspects of a job that other people have considered to be important. If a small improvement in any one of these were possible, which one would you most want it to be?

    Which would be next most important to you?
    Please continue choosing the cards in order of importance.
    Ensure that repondent orders all cards.
    Prandy *et al.*, *White-Collar Work*, Macmillan, 1984

Question 31 provides a good example of ways of *scaling* responses to questions.

recent growth and relatively high mobility, and those of old established, though small scale, industrial firms', we would have to question whether the sample would give a picture applicable to firms in the Midlands and the North.

Each white-collar worker was interviewed and for this purpose an interview schedule had to be drawn up, which could be used by the various different interviewers. In Fig. 6.3 is a reproduction of a small part of the questionnaire used. The questions demonstrate further techniques which can be utilised to produce quantifiable data.

Field work

The contacting of eighty-seven firms by letter and the initial discussions with management, constituted a substantial part of the fieldwork before the actual research proper was undertaken. When the firms had been selected then the job of interviewing the 1,924 individuals could be undertaken. It is worth noting in passing that this phase of the research process can be very expensive and take a considerable amount of time. Each interview lasted between thirty and forty minutes. Prior to this each respondent was expected to complete a checklist of questions related to their work.

Results

The actual results of this study are not of immediate concern to us. However the method of analysing the data is. The quantitative nature of the research is clear from the use of the interview schedule that deliberately tried to quantify concepts like interaction at work, relationships with employees, job security, work satisfaction etc. It is even more underlined by the use of a statstistical method on the results called 'path analysis'. How this works is beyond the scope of this book. It is a method that allows the researcher to establish a correlation between a number of variables at the same time, and to see how they interact with each other. In other words their research method enabled them to 'capture' an aspect of social reality relating to work satisfaction, and to express it in rigorous mathematical terms.

Hypotheses and theory

In the concluding section of *White-Collar Work,* the authors are able to show the impact of the social structure and social situation on the way the individual perceives his own situation. They stress that the 'individual', must be seen in terms of the 'social'.

> What emerges from our analysis of these expectations is that the great majority of our respondents are, with regard to the levels of rewards that they think they ought to get, highly constrained by what they are actually getting. What differences do exist, seem to derive from a belief that others, whom they consider to be much like themselves are receiving more than they are, and not as a result of comparisons with groups differently located.
>
> Prandy *et al., op. cit.*

The research circle is then completed as they go on to discuss the implications of their research in relation to theory in general, particularly with reference to class structure, class formation and reproduction of class.

White-Collar Work, as a type of sociological research, falls firmly towards the quantitative end of the scale, and while recognising the role of the individual, tends to adopt a macrosociological concern with social structure. Unlike Goldthorpe and Lockwood's *The Affluent Worker,* they did not incorporate more open ended qualitative research techniques in their work, and this more *humanistic* dimension is therefore missing.

Deciphering field research

This example illustrates how research can be 'deciphered'. By analysing the procedures employed by the researchers it is easier to assess what they have done and how valid their research is. It is not the purpose of this book to make a specific judgement about *White-Collar Work.* Rather it is used as an example of the first steps that must be taken for such a judgement to be made. The approach to qualitative research (although it employs theories and fieldwork and may operationalise concepts) has to be somewhat different. Rose suggests five steps in making such an evaluation (see Fig. 6.4).

Fig 6.4 **Deciphering field research**
Rose suggests the following steps for deciphering field
work and qualitative data.

1 What was the **natural history** of the research? Outline
the original purposes of the research, how the research
developed over time, field work role, field relations and
so on.
2 What **data** were collected and by what methods (observations, interviews and conversations, documents etc.)?
How were notes kept, and was any tape-recording done?
3 How was the **sampling** done? To what extent was it
accidental, theoretical and so on. . .?
4 How was the **data analysis** done? How are the data
summarised and presented in the report (illustrations,
extracts from interviews etc.) and how have these data
been selected for presentation?
5 What **results** are presented? Here, one must identify the
author's objective in the report (theory-building, description of some kind, etc.). What concepts and categories are presented? Which of these are discovered from the
data, and which were preexisting? Which are participant
concepts and which are theoretical concepts? What
theories or hypotheses are built?
Rose, 1982

In step 5, when Rose talks of 'participant concepts' he is
referring to concepts used by members of the group being
studied to explain or describe their own situation. These
need to be separated from 'theoretical concepts' developed
by the researcher.

To evaluate such research Rose argues it is necessary in
addition to assess whether the authors' *results* are consistent with
the *data* they have presented. This should be carefully analysed
for each *concept* in the research. The theory and hypotheses
presented need to be checked carefully against the *empirical
evidence* that is related to them. The *sampling procedures* have to be

examined. How far can *generalisations* be made on the basis of the group/sample studied?

This method of evaluation can be applied to the accounts of qualitative research given in Chapter 5. Further descriptions of the work of Humphreys, Whyte, Becker, Liebow, Willis and others who have used qualitative techniques are given in other texts although where possible their original work should be referred to (see Project 1 page 102).

7 Research, values and objectivity

'Facts' and 'values'

In looking at the methodology of sociology we have repeatedly come up against the question of objectivity. Some have argued that it is on this point that the question of whether sociology is scientific or not has to be assessed. In this final chapter of our analysis section we will draw some of the threads together. Our basic argument will be that neither sociology nor the natural sciences can be considered ultimately as 'value free'. Indeed sociology, dealing as it does with people who have motives and reasons for doing things, must fundamentally be concerned with values.

Scientific objectivity

Much natural science would fail if its measurements were not precise and its models and descriptions were not devised and presented in a neutral way. The scientific process operates in such a way as to develop a congruence or close similarity between the models it produces and the reality it is studying. The laws of magnetism or the description of the structure of the heart are formulated in accord with what the scientist discovers, rather than what the scientist may desire the world to be like. As we have suggested earlier in the book, the findings of scientists are verified by other scientists repeating their research. The community of scientists helps ensure the necessary objectivity of the scientific method. Science, seen in this non-problematic way, establishes *facts* and *laws*.

Social facts and negotiated meanings

Durkheim assumed that society had 'social facts' which were real and measurable in a similar way to the facts of natural science. However there is a great difference between the conscious world of human beings and the un-selfconscious natural world. As Hughes graphically puts it: 'The social sciences, however they may ape the natural sciences, have forever to face the difficulties posed by the fact that their subject matter has a voice'. (Hughes, 1980). This is another formulation of the useful dictum of Schutz: 'Science has concepts about objects, but social science has concepts about objects that have concepts'.

People have values. They have beliefs about what is morally right or wrong that influence their behaviour. These beliefs and values and the actions they affect, arise in part through day to day interactions and negotiations. Sociologists cannot ignore this aspect of society in their studies, whether under the heading of 'meanings' or 'ideology'. However, whether such value systems and attitudes can really be objectively measured is a very debatable point.

A 'value free' methodology

There are various different ways in which sociologists have claimed objectivity for their science. For Durkheim, objectivity was there in the 'social facts' that awaited discovery. These facts could be ascertained in an unbiased way through careful scientific study. His classic work on suicide was an attempt to demonstrate the objective manner in which the operation of social forces could be studied.

Two other contrasting approaches to value freedom have come from Marx and Weber.

Marx and marxism

In the marxist approach, economic relationships in society are seen as objective facts. Within any society there are those who own the means of creating wealth – the means of production – like farmland or factories, and those who have to work for them, or sell their labour. This basic *relationship to the means of production* is an objective reality that largely determines other apsects of society. Marx maintained that to a degree certain intellectuals were able to grasp this reality and see the real reasons behind historical change and the structure of society. This view would be unbiased and undistorted by *ideology*. Generally the working classes were unable to see this reality because their beliefs and values were manipulated by the bourgeois class through their control of ideology (beliefs and justifications). The falseness of these ideologies and the social structures they supported would be revealed by a true science of society.

Weber and the 'ideal type'

Weber's approach differed from Marx because he did not accept economic factors as the real or ultimate basis of reality. While he recognised the importance of social structure, his social action approach necessitated an awareness of people's interpretations and meanings. He did not see the social world as containing objective facts, rather it was a structure sustained – in part at least – by subjective understanding. However, although Weber does emphasise the subjective aspect of society, he did insist strongly that it was possible for sociology to apply a *value free methodology*. This revolved around his concept of the 'ideal type' (see Fig. 7.1). The model or paradigm implied by the ideal type could be used in a completely objective manner, even though it was 'chosen' or constructed by the social scientist and was providing insight into the highly subjective social world. The social scientist could not be satisfied with a simple description of cause and effect (as with the laws of natural science). What was required was an answer to *why* people do things. This understanding Weber called *Verstehen*. As Lewis puts it: 'One must put oneself in the other people's place, try to experience their objectives and values. It is thus that we create an 'ideal type' for any society or activity that we want to understand. And we do so only in terms of its goals, its values, its motives.'

Weber argued that the social scientist could be value free in his method while necessarily being immersed in values in terms of choice of subject matter or constructing an 'ideal type'. Steven Lukes expands this argument by pointing out that however careful we are with methodology, values will necessarily creep in. As Pratt puts it, in discussing Lukes's ideas: 'the inquirer's conclusions are *necessarily* impregnated with his values'. Concepts like 'power', Lukes argues, have to be defined (operationised). When we do so our values must inevitably be incorporated because, for example, a marxist definition of power will be different from a 'liberal' or 'conservative' one.

Fig 7.1 **The 'ideal type'**
The concept of an 'ideal type' as developed by Weber is closely linked to his belief in the possibility of a 'value free' sociology. The 'ideal type' is a model of society or its institutions or its processes. It is not ideal in the sense of being best or most moral. Rather it is a key to understanding, an aid in the process of making sense of the complexities of society. In studying bureaucracy, Weber developed an 'ideal type' that emphasised the features of rationality, efficiency and order, that he saw as being the essential aspects of bureaucratic systems. His 'ideal type' was not a hypothesis to be tested, nor was it an average of the characteristics of bureaucracies, it was rather a system of related ideas to help the sociologist understand what he was studying by investigating its key features. It allowed the sociologists to make sense of a part of the complexities of the social world. Weber applied his method to a number of aspects of modern society, most notably **capitalism** itself and one of its main causes, as Weber saw it, **ascetic protestantism.**

The 'ideal type' allows for a value free sociology because it can be used as a methodological tool to analyse society. It highlights what to look for. In other words it is a value free method. However as John Lewis points out:

> It is a complete mistake to image that Weber excludes values from his system. . . What he objects to is that, having constructed our model, we then judge its working by an outside and different value system which could have been the inner goal motivation and principle of quite another model.
>
> J. Lewis, *Max Weber and Value Free Sociology,*
> Lawrence and Wishart, 1975, p.53

Lewis is suggesting that Weber was aware we select and construct 'ideal types' in accordance with our judgement about what is relevant; however once constructed they must (and can) be applied objectively.

Can science be objective?

Before we despair over whether sociology can produce a reliable and reasonably unbiased description and explanation of society, we need to take a critical look at the actual operations of natural science itself. Perhaps the objectivity so cherished as an ideal by these sciences, is more apparent than real. Sociology in recognising (a) the subjectivity of the research process and (b) the intertwining complexities of social reality, may be informing us about the way knowledge is generated in *all* sciences.

Scientific community and culture

In Fig. 7.2 we adapt and add to the description of making sense of the world developed in the first chapter (see Figures 1.2 and 1.3 on pages 7 and 8). The suggestion is that the whole process of the production of knowledge, whether the 'hard' sciences or the social sciences, takes place in a cultural and value laden context. As we have already pointed out, scientists refer their findings to their scientific community. This is part of the scientific method and enables further testing and replication. However the community is a *social* entity. It has its own beliefs and values and its

Figure 7.2

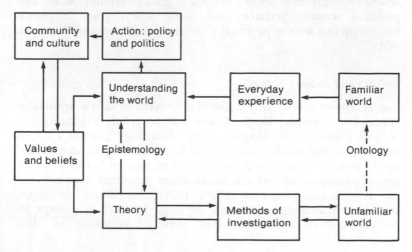

own power structures. It can partly determine the success or failure of a young scientist's career. In general it will defend the prevailing paradigm of the day and react strongly to those whose work provides a significant challenge.

The world of science, with its Cartesian, materialist outlook, is intimately linked to the achievement-orientated culture so characteristic of western industrial society. Some would maintain that this produces great pressures on the scientist to publish and make 'breakthroughs'; so much so that they turn to fraud. C. Burt's work on IQ, where he 'cooked' his figures, is a case in point but it may be more widespread than generally acknowledged.

Other limatations on science (and also sociology) are ethical questions of what knowlege can be pursued and what experiments undertaken. There is also the issue of who pays the scientist's salary. As many scientists work for large corporations or military establishments, they are far from free to 'seek knowledge for knowledge's sake'.

Policy and applications

The information created by scientific research is often used to influence policy decisions. The knowledge produced by the sciences and the knowledge of society (whether from social science or 'common sense') is used to justify certain policies and political actions. Science, and social science, are therefore caught up in a web of political evaluations whether they like it or not.

Politics and power

Social science is *necessarily* a political activity, or so it is argued by some. For example, Roger Gomm, in an article exploring the role of values in sociology, writes: 'Sociology is itself a social activity, carried out by real people in a real world and this real world is one characterised by conflicts of interest between social groups, some of whom are much more powerful than others.' (R. Gomm, in Meighan *et al.,* 1979). Sociology, therefore, produces knowledge that can be used by certain groups in society to their advantage. This view of sociology as 'shot through with issues of value' and 'underwriting views of social reality which are held by and convenient to those who have power' is in marked contrast to the image of value-free sociology so often, as Gomm points out, found in the introductory text-books.

Alvin Gouldner, in his paper *Anti-Minotaur: the myth of value-free sociology,* was one of the first to attack this comfortable but erroneous view, that social science could be as free of prejudice as the natural sciences claim to be. However, in a later article, *The Sociologist as Partisan,* he vehemently criticises Howard Becker for his belief that sociology cannot be 'uncontaminated by personal and political sympathies'. He chides Becker for his stated wish to study the social world from the point of view of the 'underdog'. He claims that Becker is too much of a romantic: the 'great white hunter who has bravely risked the perils of the urban jungle to bring back an exotic specimen.' Gouldner maintains that sociology must not be allowed to drift into a situation of complete relativism, where it is arbitary whose meaning system we work from or 'whose side we are on'. Sociologists should be objective in terms of impartial judgement and have what he calls personal authenticity. 'Personal authenticity or awareness exists when the sociologist is capable of admitting the factuality even of things that violate his own hopes and wishes' (A. Gouldner, *For Sociology,* Allen Lane, 1973, p.59). Gouldner insists that sociologists must not allow themselves to become complacent, assured of a comfortable professional life, and lacking the drive to do something about human suffering.

PART 3

Statistical data and documentary readings

8 Statistics

In June 1984, just before a by-election, the National Opinion Poll (NOP) conducted a survey of Portsmouth voters. The results they came up with were:

Conservative	43%
Labour	31%
SDP/Liberal	25%

These statistics were based on a survey of about 1,000 potential voters. We would expect that as the actual election was only a few days away, the poll would have given a good indication of voting on the day itself. It didn't. It was completely wrong as we show in Reading 1. This would be merely amusing, if it were not for the fact that polls such as these also tend to influence the political process, through, for example, the so-called 'band wagon' effect.

The statistical approach is of course primarily associated with a positivist/quantitative position in sociology. The very representation of aspects of social reality in a numerical form, tends to suggest 'hard social facts' in society are there to be measured.

In effect, very few sociologists do not use statistics. However it is as well to realise that they are *not* simple facts. They are created as part of a social process. The extracts that we give in this section illustrate this, with particular reference to deviance. Before introducing them we will consider the process of producing statistics and the problematic nature of statistics in other sociological areas.

To simplify matters somewhat, we can say that statistics tend to be produced either as a result of a specific research project (primary data) or they have been collected for other purposes, often by government agencies (secondary data). In each case we would suggest that the statistics are produced in a social context. This is illustrated in Fig. 8.1. However the statistics are collected,

Figure 8.1

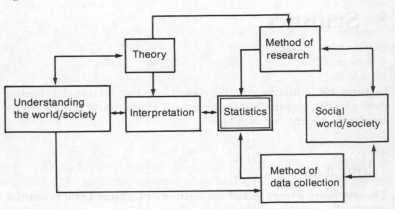

or for whatever purpose, we can suggest that the prior 'understanding of the world' will tend to influence the process. This understanding will also impinge on any interpretation. To give one example, as men are considered (in common sense terms and in much sociological theory) to be 'head of the household', the *class* position of a family is based on the man's occupation, *even* if the wife works outside the home, and is in a 'higher' occupation.

Statistics can be very political. The developed West likes to publish, in governmental reports, what it gives as aid to the Third World. What is rarely published next to these figures, is the amount (usually much greater) that the West gets back from the Third World in terms of profit on trade and interest payments.

In domestic politics, the relative results of grammar schools as compared to comprehensives *can* show grammar schools do 'much better' in terms of 'A' level results. However when these statistics are adjusted to account for comprehensives which are 'creamed' of their best pupils by grammar schools in the same area, the results from both types of school prove to be much the same. These statistics are not 'facts' that speak for themselves; they have to be used cautiously and assessed critically.

The recent work of both Douglas and Atkinson has shown that suicide statistics are far from being as factual as we might initially expect. They strongly criticise Durkheim's classic study *Suicide,* on the grounds that he did not treat the statistics as social creations, which themselves fluctuate because of social factors, like coroner interpretations.

Steven Box has analysed how statistics about crime are produced and Reading 2 is an adaptation of a diagram which summarises his ideas on how the process takes place. The various statistics like rates of arrest, numbers of charges, convictions etc. are all products of social interactions and decisions. Different decisions will produce different rates. The rates are not 'facts'.

The table in Reading 3 shows how this process of decision taking can translate into statistics. These figures are from Anne Campbell's study of female delinquency. Figures showing the numbers of girls convicted of offences like theft, criminal damage, burglary etc. would show a lower rate than boys. However when the proportion of girls cautioned as compared to boys, is considered, the reason becomes clearer. It is not necessarily that they commit less crime. Rather the police seem to respond differently.

In the final reading in this section, Bottomley and Coleman show how 'cuffing' is a not uncommon police practice. As it decreases, so the crime rate may appear to increase, even though no more crime may actually be being committed.

Reading 1

This table shows the result of the NOP survey compared with the actual vote by electors in June 1984. As polls appear to be playing an increasingly important and controversial part in current political life, it is well to reflect on the circumstances in which they are produced, and the causes of inaccuracies (if indeed they are inaccurate).

Table 8.1 Comparison of forecast by the NOP with the actual results of the
Portsmouth by-election

	NOP	Result
Conservative	43%	34.3%
Labour	31%	26.5%
SDP/LIB	25%	37.6%

Questions

1 Suggest reasons why there are differences between the poll
and the actual election result.
2 Suggest ways in which a sample might be selected to produce
an accurate poll at not too great a cost.

Reading 2

This diagram is adapted from Steven Box. It starts from the 'dark
figure' of acts of deviance actually committed. What this in fact is
can never be known with certainty. Note that the phrase used is
'acts of deviance' because they may or may not be seen as crimes
as such. The police can decide to caution or to arrest the suspect
they have apprehended. If they make an arrest, this can result in a
charge at the station or just a warning. All the way through
decisions are being made by people according to how they
interpret the situation (see Fig 8.2).

Questions

1 Why might the 'status of the complainant' make a difference
to the police decision?
2 What factors could influence the police to caution or to release
a suspect?
3 What methods could be used to gain a more reliable idea of
how the 'dark figure' of crime and deviance changes year by
year?

Reading 3

This table, quoted by Anne Campbell, is taken from Home
Office figures for 1977. It refers to those who were apprehended

Figure 8.2 The social construction of official statistics (adapted from S. Box, **Deviance, Reality and Society,** *1981)*

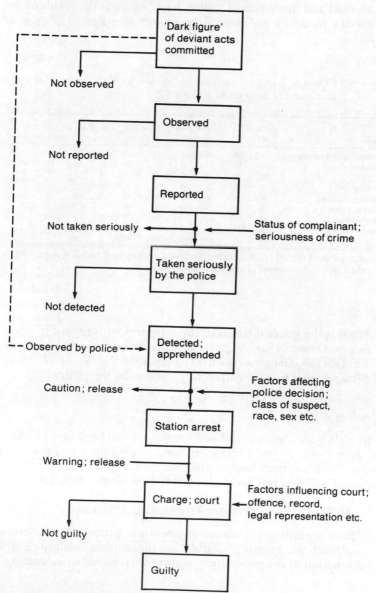

by the police, cautioned, and then no further action taken. These figures are presented as a percentage of those who were only cautioned and those found guilty. Each figure is the result of the decisions made by police officers about whether to charge or not.

Table 8.2 Offenders cautioned for indictable offences as a percentage of all those cautioned and those found guilty, 1977

Offence	All ages		10–13 years		14–16 years		17–20 years		21+ years	
	M	F	M	F	M	F	M	F	M	F
Violence against the person	8	20	56	61	24	35	2	7	4	11
Sexual offences	33	56	83	83	64	100	54	60	13	46
Burglary	15	29	47	63	18	31	1	3	1	4
Robbery	3	6	23	25	6	11	–	–	–	–
Theft and handling	24	34	76	87	43	63	3	5	4	11
Fraud and forgery	6	11	70	79	38	52	3	5	2	6
Criminal damage	16	19	60	69	29	38	2	5	2	6
Other offences	1	7	69	95	30	53	3	5	2	3
Total indictable offences	19	31	67	85	34	58	3	5	3	10

Source: Home Office 1977, Criminal Statistics for England and Wales quoted by Cambell in *Girl Delinquents*, Basil Blackwell, 1981

Questions

1 What is the general trend in these figures with regard to age?
2 Suggest reasons for the pattern of statistics for sexual offences.
3 Explain the change in all the figures after the age of 17.
4 Why are girls treated differently to boys by the police?

Reading 4

The police are under social and organisational pressures in much of their work. A good 'clear-up rate' is obviously important to them. As this extract shows, this can lead to practices which *may* be good policing but produces distortions in the statistics.

UNDER THE ARM AND OFF THE RECORD: 'CUFFING'

These preliminary comments upon the procedures of 'criming' and 'no criming' would be incomplete without some discussion of the procedure commonly referred to as 'cuffing'.

The importance of this custom for our research is that incidents which could technically be the subject of a crime report are not initially put down on paper for official record. This practice can often give strategic advantages to the officer concerned, quite apart from its long term effects on crime rates, and more obliquely, the clear-up rate. For example, an incident which looks unlikely to be detected may be 'cuffed', saving the officer some unwelcome paper work, thereby keeping an extra unit out of the crime rate, and making the clear-up rate more respectable if such a practice is frequently used. According to senior officers we spoke to, who often referred to the practice as 'keeping something under the arm', the practice might also occur in offences that were highly promising in terms of detection, and still serve a strategic purpose for the individual officer, e.g. the offence could be used against the offender at a later date to extract valuable information or an admission to a more serious crime, or in a rather different way, it might be cuffed in the initial stages so that the officer could save the probable arrest for himself rather than hand it 'on a plate' to one of his colleagues (most likely from the CID!). To understand this point it is important to realise that in most cases a member of the uniformed branch will be the first to the scene of the crime and will therefore conduct initial enquiries and begin the crime report. Unless there is a quick arrest at or near the scene, the document, and thus responsibility for further investigation will then be handed over to the CID. This, of course, is just one small indication of the ambivalent feelings of the uniformed branch towards the CID.

Senior officers we spoke to appeared to agree that cuffing had steadily declined in recent years. One described the period between the wars as equivalent to a 'golden age' of cuffing. Another said that 'everything' was now put on a crime report, although it was only because of other context-bound remarks that one could possibly know what he meant by 'everything'. He also speculated that the rising crime rate within his area during the 1970s might be due mainly to the decline in the incidence of the practice.

Bottomley, K., and Coleman, C., *Understanding Crime Rates*, Gower, 1981

Questions

1 What does 'cuffing' actually mean?
2 What research procedures could be undertaken to study 'cuffing'?
3 Assess the argument that 'crime statistics tell us more about law enforcers than law breakers'.

9 Theories, values and research

The intimate relationship between theory and method has been a constant theme of this book. The whole process of making sense of social phenomena does not take place inside some sort of conceptual vacuum. Rather, the types of questions the researcher asks and the sort of research strategy adopted, will tend to be influenced by, at the very least, their common sense understanding of society, if not by some overall theory. For example, the research into schools and the labour market by Willis, in *Learning to Labour,* was not a haphazard choice. Willis saw the school as a vital part of the mechanism that a capitalist society employed, to protect middle class jobs for middle class children. More than this, it ensured that there were sufficient working class youths keen to escape from school into the mind-deadening unskilled manual labouring work. The method he used – ethnography – fitted in with his interactionist approach, although this was in the context of a marxist outlook on society.

It is this theme which Ackroyd and Hughes discuss in Reading 5. They maintain that research methods cannot be seen as so many tools in a tool-box. It is not an arbitrary choice whether one decides to undertake a social survey rather than do participant observation. They stress the point that a method is most productive when it is used in concert with an appropriate theoretical outlook.

Two contrasting extracts follow which take this discussion a step further. A sociologist who adopts a marxist viewpoint tends to aver that certain relationships will exist in society because they are fundamentally part of social reality. Ever since a surplus has been produced there has been an owning group and a group that has to sell its labour power. According to Berger and Kellner in Reading 6, such an ideological outlook has tended to distort the methodology used by some marxist sociologists. They would argue that in this case the domination of method by theory is such as to render the research quite unscientific. It become merely dogmatism.

The contrast between this extract and that of Sherman and

Wood in Reading 7, could not be stronger. They quote Marx as saying about the fundamental ideas and axioms that they hold to be true, that 'the premises from which we begin are not arbitary ones, not dogmas . . .' Indeed far from being merely theoretical constructs they quote Marx as saying 'These premises can thus be verified in a purely empirical way'.

The debate about objectivity and marxist analysis can only be raised briefly here and cannot be resolved in these few pages. However it is worth reflecting on Popper's warning that we can never test a theory which is referring to changes on a world wide scale.

In Reading 8 with which we conclude this section, Glaser and Strauss explain what they see as the importance of grounded theory. Theory should be inductively generated, they argue. In other words it should arise from a bedrock of solid research data. Their work is a response in particular to the 'grand theorists' like Parsons.

Reading 5

In the first reading in this section the common theme that methods cannot really be divorced from theory, is explored from the methodological point of view.

METHODS AND SOCIAL THEORY

The orthodox view sees methods of research more or less as tools and there are two closely related variants of this worth mentioning. The first is the 'nature of the problem' view, according to which there are methods ready and waiting for any research occasion. Research is simply a matter of defining, relatively explicitly, the nature of our problem in order to undertake appropriate research. All a researcher has to do is look on the shelf containing methods of research and select the appropriate one for his research problem. The second and related variant, which is scarcely more defensible, is the 'nature of the method' approach, which suggests that there are only certain limited potentialities in particular methods and, to this extent we must recognise that certain methods can discover only certain things. To some degree this is true, but the reasons for it are complex.

Both of these variants contain kernels of truth about the nature of research methods. But the major fault we find with them is that they present a view in which theoretical considerations are too divorced from technical ones. While it is often the case that methods are treated as if they were tools in a tool-box ready and waiting to be used for their appropriate job, it is vitally important that any aspiring methodologist does not take this too seriously, but tries to understand the kind of presupposition underpinning methods we have been talking about.

One consequence of the 'tool-box' view is a tendency to use data generally without too much regard for the theoretical issues involved in their production. There are 'facts' in the world, recorded in various ways, and all a researcher has to do is gather those relevant to the problem at hand. It matters little whether the 'facts' or the 'data' are produced by a questionnaire survey, found in a document, or the result of observation. Admittedly, there may be problems of a technical nature, but these are treated as of little theoretical moment.

However, by contrast, some research methods and the data they generate, develop within a particular theoretical tradition or approach. These represent theory–specific uses of a method. The distinction between generic and theory–specific methods is important though often overlooked by methodologists. It is important because theory–specific methods are at their most effective when used within their appropriate theoretical context. Outside of the appropriate theoretical context, theory–specific methods can be more of a liability than an asset. Such a user is likely to draw conclusions from the data which are not warranted by the theoretical presuppositions of the methods. The line between generic and theory–specific data and methods is not always easy to draw and is a moving one as we shall see. The method of participant observation, for example, was mostly developed within the symbolic interactionist approach to sociology, and has been refined almost exclusively by researchers adopting this framework. It has been in the main theory–specific. By contrast, the survey was developed as a generic method for use to practical ends. Only subsequently was it rendered more theory–specific, and has passed through several theory–specific types. In other words, methods have a habit of crossing the distinction between generic and theory–specific in response to developments within the social science disciplines.

Ackroyd, S., and Hughes, J.A.,
Data Collection in Context, Longman, 1981

Questions

1 Explain what is meant by a 'tool-box' view of methods.
2 Why should certain theory–specific methods 'be at their most effective when used in their appropriate theoretical context'?
3 Discuss the advantages and disadvantages of using a social survey in sociological research.

Reading 6

The 'way of seeing' by marxist sociology is influenced, say Berger and Kellner, by its 'ideological animus'. By this they mean the ideas, values and outlook that are built into or enshrined in the way that marxists view the world. The authors are using a Weberian social action approach to criticise marxist sociology.

MARXIST IDEOLOGY

. . . Marxist propositions on the correlation between capitalism and imperialism are 'researchable' by means of social-scientific methods that we would fully approve of; using such methods, specific Marxist hypotheses on this matter could be either supported or falsified. Rather, the boundary is methodological. Marxism, because of its deeply rooted connection between utopian and scientific relevances, carries an ideological animus that ongoingly interferes with the sociological 'way of seeing'. Frequently, this animus blinds and distorts the Marxist sociologist to crucial elements of social reality. Take, for example, the bizarre quest of Marxist sociologists in Western countries for an empirically unavailable 'proletariat': because there was an ideological requirement for this class to exist, the most ingenious ways were devised in order to 'discover' (put brutally, to invent) it. Or, for another example, take the remarkable inability of Marxist sociology to shed any light on the social reality of existing socialist societies – a reality that, of course, is very hard to reconcile with the ideology. In the most serious cases (and by no means only in the case of the legitimating ideologists in the Soviet Union and other socialist societies that tolerate something called 'sociology') this attitude leads to closed, dogmatic systems of thought, which are the direct antithesis of science.

In these instances, 'sociology' becomes a deduction from the *a priori* principles given in the ideology, an unfolding of a 'truth' already known. One then 'knows' from the beginning what one is going to find; not surprisingly, one then proceeds to find it. Again, there are extreme cases (though not on that account, rare ones). But even if this or that variant is not yet dogmatic in this sense, there is always a totalistic tendency. The reason for this is, quite simply, the Marxist idea of a theory that will be an all-embracing system – an ideal that bears an odd resemblance to the totalistic ideal of positivism.

From Berger, P.L., and Kellner, H.,
Sociology Reinterpreted, Penguin, 1981

Reading 7

The contrast to the previous reading could not be more striking. Far from there being 'ideological pollution' in marxist methods of research, Sherman and Wood see Marx's work as strongly based in empirical research. His works 'present an enormous amount of facts' although 'he wraps his facts together in a tight theoretical framework'. For them Marx strikes the right balance between 'theories–and–facts'.

MARX'S MATERIALISM

Marx's materialist method directs sociologists to derive their knowledge from observation, experiment, and participation in the real material and social world. Marx notes: 'The premises from which we begin are not arbitrary ones, not dogmas, but real premises from which abstraction can only be made in the imagination.' By 'real premises' he clearly means our knowledge about live human beings in the context of their actual life and work situations. Marx concludes that 'These premises can thus be verified in a purely empirical way.'

'Idealists', in terms of a method of sociology, are those who think that knowledge of society can be obtained by some route other than the hard work of empirical observation. Although most sociologists would now agree with the empirical aspect of the materialist approach, there are always some newer versions of idealism or rationalism advocated in sociology (some of which call themselves 'critical' or even 'radical').

In spite of Marx's strong commitment to empirical research, many traditional critics (such as Karl Popper) still claim that Marx based himself on rationalist, *a priori* theories and merely collected a few facts for illustration. Yet Marx's *Capital* and his other works present an enormous amount of facts.

Perhaps these critics are led astray because Marx rejects positivist empiricism (separation of facts from theory) and wraps his facts together in a tight theoretical framework. Marxists and radicals have always attacked empiricism or positivism just as much as they have attacked idealism or rationalism. Empiricism is criticized on two grounds, both discussed above in some detail. First, one cannot choose problems, collect facts, or interpret facts without a theoretical framework. Contrary to the empiricists, theory and fact are inseparable parts of one continuing scientific process. We cannot do without theory in empirical research, and if a traditional sociologist claims to collect facts with no theory, then he or she is likely to be just using a theory implicitly and unconsciously instead of explicitly and consciously. Furthermore, his or her theory is usually the dominant social ideology or set of social myths. Second, in the practice of sociological research, this means not only unconscious acceptance of the dominant ideology, but also concentration on easily quantifiable smaller problems and neglect of the larger controversial problems.

Marx's materialism thus rejects both the rationalist approach of pure theory without any factual basis and the empiricist approach of collecting numerous facts without much theoretical framework. Rather, Marx finds the need for a continuous process in which the sociologist begins by considering the known 'theories–and–facts'. Then, through empirical research within a theoretical framework, the sociologist arrives at a set of 'new–theories–and–new–facts'.

Sherman, H.J., and Wood, J.L.,
Sociology: traditional and radical perspectives,
Harper and Row, 1982

Questions

1 Explain the difference between 'empiricism' and 'idealism'.
2 Is the existence of a 'proletariat' essentially a theoretical issue or an empirical one?
3 What is meant by the notion that Marx 'wraps his facts together in a tight theoretical framework'?
4 Discuss the contention that marxist sociology is an 'unfolding of a 'truth' already known'.

Reading 8

Glaser and Strauss attempt to avoid accusations of ideological distortion by arguing for theory which 'fits and works' because it is developed out of empirical research. In this case the facts will not be wrapped in a tight theoretical framework, rather the theory will be generated from examination of data.

GROUNDED THEORY

To generate theory that fills this large order, we suggest as the best approach an initial, systematic discovery of the theory from the data of social research. Then one can be relatively sure that the theory will fit and work. And since the categories are discovered by examination of the data, laymen involved in the area to which the theory applies will usually be able to understand it, while sociologists who work in other areas will recognise an understandable theory linked with the data of a given area.

Theory based on data can usually not be completely refuted by more data or replaced by another theory. Since it is too intimately linked to data, it is destined to last despite its inevitable modification and reformulation. The most striking examples are Weber's theory of bureaucracy and Durkheim's theory of suicide. These theories have endured for decades, stimulating a variety of research and study, constantly exciting students and professors alike to try to modify them by clever ways of testing and reformulation. In contrast, logically deduced theories based on ungrounded assumptions, such as some well-known ones on the 'social system' and on 'social action' can lead their followers far astray in trying to advance sociology. However, grounded theories – which take hard study of much data – are worth the precious time and focus of all of us in our research, study and teaching.

In contrasting grounded theory with logico-deductive theory and discussing and assessing their relative merits in ability to fit and work (predict, explain, and be relevant), we have taken the position that the adequacy of a theory for sociology today cannot be divorced from the process by which it is generated. Thus one canon for judging the usefulness of a theory is how it was generated – and we suggest that it is likely to be a better theory to the degree that it has been inductively developed from social research. We also believe that other canons for assessing a theory, such as logical consistence, clarity, parsimony, density, scope, integration, as well as its fit and its ability to work, are also significantly dependent on how the theory was generated. They are not, as some theorists of a logico-deductive persuasion would claim, completely independent of the processes of generation.

Glaser, B., and Strauss, A.,
The Discovery of Grounded Theory,
Weidenfeld and Nicholson, 1968

Questions

1 What is 'grounded theory'.
2 Explain what is meant by the 'adequacy of a theory'?
3 Assess the role of theory and method in the generation of sociological understanding.

10 Research methods

In this final chapter, we will look in greater detail at some facts of the research process. The first document, reproduced in Reading 9 shows some questions from the interview schedule used in the General Household Survey (GHS), 1981. This is a very detailed survey, as the questions demonstrate. It provides a lot of factual information that can be used to assess certain sociological theories.

In great contrast to the GHS, is Seabrook's investigation of working class childhood, by using oral histories. Although the extract in Reading 10 is short, it gives something of the 'flavour' of the material from the 20 or so interviews which Seabrook quotes in his book. The story is told in their own words. We are largely left to draw the sociological conclusions ourselves. This approach is associated with an ethnographic/interpretist perspective.

Another book that takes a similar approach is *The View in Winter* by Ronald Blythe. This studies old age through the eyes of the old and those who are involved with them. Again the technique is largely to allow the words and perceptions of those interviewed to build up the picture.

A more structured approach was taken by Becker in his study of marihuana users. Reading 11 explains how he approached his interviewees, and the sort of hypothesis he was working on. Becker has been very influential in establishing the interpretive approach to sociology, although, as we saw in the our discussion of Gouldner in Chapter 7, he has not been without his critics. In the extract Becker considers the problem of surveying, and also the issue of how his hypothesis can be validated. While research into deviance and deviants has been a strong thread in the history of sociology, it has its own particular problems. Laurie Taylor has recently completed a study of East End crooks, called *In The Underworld* (1984). In reviewing the book, Clancy Segal suggested Taylor may well have been misled. Taylor had been introduced to this underworld by armed robber, turned sociologist, John McVicar.

'You sound so fucking silly,' con man Geoff complains to Taylor. 'Always putting in those clever little comments. Why don't you listen a bit more and keep quiet until you have something to say?' Taylor disarmingly emphasises how the crooks graudally tore down his academic detachment. But I don't believe for a moment that anyone was telling the truth. The crooks would have been crazy to trust Taylor, even on the say-so of McVicar.

C. Segal, in *The Guardian,* 1984

The problem of being misled may have affected no less a personage than the famous anthropologist, Margaret Mead. Her book *Coming of Age in Samoa,* is probably the most widely read serious anthropological study. It has been enormously influential. But Freeman in Reading 12 shows how young Samoan girls in the 1920s may have spun myths and tales to Mead, that have had repercussions far beyond their wildest fancies. Mead's book was very popular, and had an impact on the thinking of a whole generation. The important question of whether cultural factors or biological ones were more important as determinants of behaviour, appeared to be settled once and for all by her findings. If she got it wrong, it is of more than minor academic interest.

Just how difficult in a social sense the whole question of conducting an interview is, is raised in Pahl and Pahl's discussion in Reading 13. Here they look at the difficulties of carrying out a formal interview with married women, when the questions themselves set a constraint. The inherent tension in the situation is very apparent.

In Reading 14 the whole issue is taken further with Oakley's reflections on interviewing about childbirth. She argues forcefully that the positivist approach to interviews, with a detached, objective and impersonal ideal, is inappropriate and ineffective. The interview relationship, with the interviewer (often male) and the interviewee (often a housewife) is constructed in accordance with a masculine and patriarchal psychological analysis of the situation. Oakley doubts if this approach is justified either in terms of accuracy of information or in terms of what is acceptable behaviour for the interviewer.

Reading 9

This example has been chosen because it shows clearly how questions can be coded and also the way inteviewers are guided as to how to fill in the schedule, and what questions to move on to.

Example of a coded interview schedule

TO ALL

Now I would like to ask you about your household's accommodation, excluding any rooms you may let or sublet   SHARED

5.	Do you have either a fixed bath or a fixed shower with hot water supply?	Yes... No ...	1 2		1
6.	Do you have a flush toilet?	Yes... No ...	1 2	▸(e) ▸Q.7	
	IF YES (a) Is the entrance to it				
	CODE inside your accommodation?............... FIRST outside your accommodation THAT but inside the building? .... APPLIES outside the building		3 = 5	▸Q.7	3 4 5
7.	How many bedrooms do you have, including bedsitting rooms and spare bedrooms? ENTER NO. ⟶		......		......
8.	Are any of them used by your household for cooking in – like a bedsitter for example?	Yes... No ...	1 2		
9.	(Apart from that) do you have a kitchen, that is a separate room in which you cook?	Yes... No ...	1 2	▸(a)&(b) ▸Q.10	1
	IF YES (a) Is the narrowest side of the kitchen less than 6½ ft wide from wall to wall?	Less than 6½ ft ... 6½ ft or more ...	1 2		
	(b) Do (any of) you ever eat meals in it or use it as a sitting room?	Yes... No ...	1 2	▸Q.10	

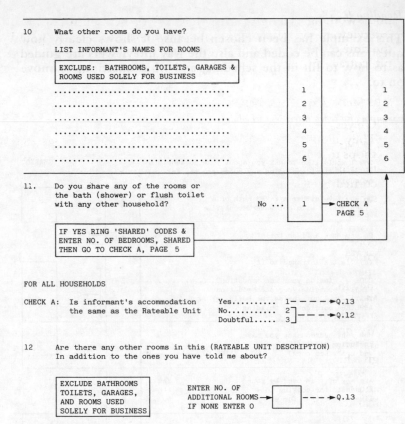

Questions

1 What sociological concepts could be measured by using data from questions like these? Would they provide a *valid* measure?
2 How would you check on the reliability of this interview schedule?
3 Discuss the value and limitations of sources of data like the GHS and *Social Trends*.

Reading 10

This extract from Seabrook's book illustrates the childhood of a poor working class girl. Mrs McIver – in her seventies when interviewed – is reflecting on her experiences in Wigan around the time of the first world war. She lives now in what used to be a pit 'cottage'.

MRS McIVER'S CHILDHOOD

Oh yes, we had a rough time. There were 17 of us; 17 children. They didn't all live. My brothers had to pinch food from shops to help feed us all. They would distribute it around, and they used our cellar to store it all. They used to get tins of corned beef, fish, ham, everything. Once they took a whole sack of flour from a shop. They didn't realise there was a hole in it; so of course the police could follow this trail of flour from the shop right to our front door. They knocked on the door, and our mother opened it. They said to her, did she know anything about any flour? She said, 'I've got no flour apart from what I use for my baking.' But of course, when they looked, they found it, and all sorts of other things as well. My brothers were sent away for that, they did time. It didn't stop them though. It was the only way to get enough to eat. My brother broke into a shop once, and there was this cat starting mewing. He strangled it to shut it up, so it wouldn't give him away. He didn't get caught that time.

We used to get our food on credit, go and pay on Thursday; and then stock up with a fresh supply for the next week. You had to pay all you owed before you could start again. Once my mother sent me to get the groceries. She hadn't got enough money to pay for them all, so she said to me, 'Now make sure you get all the stuff before you pay.' She gave me what she had, but we knew it wasn't enough. So I got all this stuff, potatoes, tinned stuff, cheese, whatever it was. Then I gave him the money I'd got from my mother. 'Me Mam sent this.' He said, 'You leave all that bloody stuff on the counter.' He was going to take it all back. I went mad. I started throwing everything around, all the tins, I threw them at the shelves where everything was all stacked up; the whole lot came crashing down. I threw the jackbut all over the shop. I was that mad, he thought I'd wreck the place. He let me take the groceries.

Seabrook, J., *Working Class Childhood*, Gollancz, 1982

Questions

1 Assess the value of acounts like this for the study of childhood.
2 'Personal documents, like diaries, and oral histories provide insight but lack analysis.' Explain and evaluate this statement.

Reading 11

Becker reflects, in this extract, on the methods he used to gain information on marihuana users. Note that although he works from an interpretive position he still is aware of the positivist arguments about the need to be scientific and to test his hypothesis.

STUDYING MARIHUANA USERS

In doing the study, I used the method of analytic induction. I tried to arrive at a general statement of the sequence of changes in individual attitude and experience which always occurred when the individual became willing and able to use marihuana for pleasure, and never occurred or had not been permanently maintained when the person was unwilling to use marihuana for pleasure. The method requires that every case collected in the research substantiate the hypothesis. If one case is encountered which does not substantiate it, the researcher is required to change the hypothesis to fit the case which has proven his original idea wrong.

To develop and test my hypothesis about the genesis of marihuana use for pleasure, I conducted fifty interviews with marihuana users. I had been a professional dance musician for some years when I conducted this study and my first interviews were with people I had met in the music business. I asked them to put me in contact with other users who would be willing to discuss their experiences with me. Colleagues working on a study of users of opiate drugs made a few interviews available to me which contained, in addition to material on opiate drugs, sufficient material on the use of marihuana to furnish a test of my hypothesis. Although in the end half of the fifty interviews were conducted with musicians, the other half covered a wide range of people, including labourers, machinists, and people in the professions. The sample is, of course, in no sense 'random'; it would not be possible to draw a random sample, since no one knows the nature of the universe from which it would have to be drawn.

In interviewing users, I focused on the history of the person's experience with marihuana, seeking major changes in his attitude toward it and in his actual use of it, and the reasons for these changes. Where it was possible and appropriate, I used the jargon of the user himself.

The theory starts with the person who has arrived at the point of willingness to try marihuana. He knows others use marihuana to 'get high', but he does not know what this means in any concrete way. He is curious about the experience, ignorant of what it may turn out to be, and afraid it may be more than he has bargained for.

Becker, H., *Outsiders,* Free Press, 1963

Questions

1 Why was it not possible to have a totally random sample of marihuana users?
2 What is the point, in this sort of research, of 'using the jargon of the user himself'?

Reading 12

The possibility that Mead 'got it wrong' caused quite a stir when Freeman's book was first published. While he has been criticised by some, his explanation does raise some serious issues about the general reliability of all interviews or use of informants, especially those that cut across cultural or sub-cultural lines.

THE MAKING OF AN ANTHROPOLOGICAL MYTH

Mead's depiction of Samoan culture, as I have shown, is marked by major errors, and her account of the sexual behaviour of Samoans by a mind-boggling contradiction, for she asserts that the Samoans have a culture in which female virginity is very highly valued, with a virginity-testing ceremony being 'theoretically observed at weddings of all ranks,' while at the same time adolescence among females is regarded as a period 'appropriate for love-making'. And, indeed, she actually describes the Samoans as making the 'demand' that a female should be 'both receptive to the advances of many lovers and yet capable of showing the tokens of virginity at marriage.' Something, it become plain at this juncture, is emphatically amiss, for surely no human population could be so cognitively disoriented as to conduct their lives in such a schizophrenic way. Nor are the Samoans remotely like this. They are, in fact, a people who traditionally value virginity highly and so disapprove of pre-marital promiscuity as to exercise a strict surveillance over the comings and goings of adolescent girls. That these values and this regime were in force in Manu'a in the mid 1920s is, furthermore, clearly established by the testimony of the Manu'ans themselves who, when I discussed this period with those who well remembered it, confirmed that the fa'aSamoa in these matters was operative then as it was both before and after Mead's brief sojourn in Ta'u. What then can have been the source of Mead's erroneous statement that in Samoa there is great premarital freedom, with promiscuity before marriage among adolescent girls, being both permitted and expected?

The explantation most consistently advanced by the Samoans themselves for the magnitude of the errors in her depiction of their culture and in particular of their sexual morality is, as Gerber has reported, 'that Mead's informants must have been telling lies in order to tease her.' Those Samoans who offer this explanation, which I have heard in Manu'a as well as in other parts of Samoa, are referring to the behaviour caller *tau fa'ase'e,* to which Samoans are much prone. *Fa'ase'e* (literally 'to cause to slip') means 'to dupe,' as in the example given by Milner, *'e fa'ase'e gofie le teine,* the girl is easily duped'; and the phrase *tau fa'ase'e* refers to the action of deliberately duping someone, a pastime that greatly appeals to the Samoans as a respite from the severities of their authoritarian society.

Freeman, D., *Margaret Mead and Samoa,* Penguin, 1983

Reading 13

Pahl and Pahl note, when trying to question people about how they saw themselves, that 'many of these questions were not successful, particularly with the women'. The ability of the respondents to express themselves in abstract terms and the dynamics of the interview situation, both seemed to be limiting factors.

THE WIFE'S INTERVIEW

The interview with the wife was primarily concerned with finding out the sort of life she led, and to what extent this, and the way she viewed it, was determined by the fact of being a manager's wife. The interview had two main sections, the first attempting to form some general picture of her ideas about herself and how these had changed over a considerable period of her life; the second asking mainly for detailed, factual accounts of some aspects of her day-to-day life.

However, to arrive at a 'hierarchy of role identities' or 'self-conceptions at appropriate stages of the life cycle' by asking people a series of questions about how they saw themselves, was a process that not only took a great deal of time, but was also frequently unproductive. During the course of the interviews the questions were approached in a number of different ways, all of which tried to avoid introducing the concept of role. Many of these questions were not successful, particularly with the women. Often the questions, however phrased, produced in response a series of adjectives which the women would use to describe themselves, such as 'ordinary' or 'patient'. These adjectives were seldom in combination with any noun other than 'woman', and generally did not refer to any particular situation. Answers tended to be along the lines 'I'm fairly ordinary' or 'I've more confidence now than I use to have'. Attempts to follow up these answers by getting the women to tie them into particular circumstances or changes in their lives also had little success, and it was difficult to enlarge on the questions without predetermining the answers. Their ideas about themselves as mothers, wives, career women and so forth, and the conflicts engendered by the differing demands of these roles were much more adequately expressed in the second half of the interview when they talked about the organisation of their home life, their attitudes to their husband's work, and their own involvements outside the home.

There was a noticeable difference in the ease with which the men and women replied to these particular questions, and it did seem that the men were much more immediately aware of conflict between their home lives and their work lives. On the one hand, the men in general were much more articulate in expressing their ideas about themselves, and appeared to be more accustomed to this type of self-analysis. For many of the women, the whole of the first section of the interview seemed too abstract, and they were frequently disconcerted by the questions, commenting that they found them difficult to answer and that they didn't spend much time thinking about themselves. Some apologised for their answers, either because they did find difficulty in expressing adequately what they wanted to say, or because they thought that what they did think was so 'uninspired' as to be of no interest. Yet others were worried that the whole procedure was too introspective to be a good thing, or that an honest self-appraisal would tend to sound immodest.

Pahl, J.M., and Pahl, R.E., *Managers and Their Wives,*
Allen Lane, 1971

Reading 14

The theme of the limitations of the interview situation is taken up by Oakley. She broke with usual practice in having a number of follow up interviews with her respondents. As she points out at the end, some were to become close friends.

INTERVIEWING WOMEN

In terms of my experience in the childbirth project, I found that interviewees very often took the initiative in defining the interviewer–interviewee relationship as something which existed beyond the limits of question–asking and answering. For example, they did not only offer the minimum hospitality of accommodating me in their homes for the duration of the interview: at 92 per cent of the interviews I was offered tea, coffee or some other drink; 14 per cent of the women also offered me a meal on at least one occasion. There was also a certain amount of interest in my own situation. What sort of person was I and how did I come to be interested in this subject?

In some cases these kind of 'respondent' reactions were evident at the first interview. More often they were generated after the second interview and an important factor here was probably the timing of the interviews. There was an average of 20 weeks between interviews 1 and 2, an average of 11 weeks between interviews 2 and 3 and an average of 15 weeks between interviews 3 and 4. Between the first two interviews most of the women were very busy. Most were still employed and had the extra work of preparing equipment/ clothes/ a room for the baby – which sometimes meant moving house. Between interviews 2 and 3 most were not out at work and, sensitised by the questions I had asked in the first two interviews to my interest in their birth experiences, probably began to associate me in a more direct way with their experiences of the transition to motherhood. At interview 2 I gave them all a stamped addressed postcard on which I asked them to write the date of their baby's birth so I would know when to re-contact them for the first postnatal interview. I noticed that this was usually placed in a prominent position (for example on the mantlepiece), to remind the women or her husband to complete it and it probably served in this way as a reminder of my intrusion into their lives. One illustration of this awareness comes from the third interview with Mary Rosen, a 25-year-old exhibition organiser: 'I thought of you after he was born, I thought she'll never believe it – a six hour labour, a 9lb 6oz baby and no forceps – and all without an epidural, although I had said to you that I wanted one.' Sixty two per cent of the women expressed a substantial and quite detailed interest in the research; they wanted to know its goals, any proposed methods for disseminating its findings, how I had come to think of it in the first place, what the attitudes of doctors I had met or collaborated with were to it and so forth. Some of the women took the initiative in contacting me to arrange the second or a subsequent interview, although I had made it clear that I would get in touch with them. Several rang up to report particularly important pieces of information about their antenatal care – in one case a distressing encounter with a doctor who told a woman keen on natural childbirth that this was 'for animals: in this hospital we give epidurals'; in another case to tell me of an ultrasound result that changed the expected date of delivery. Several also got in touch to correct or add to things they had said during an interview – for instance, one contacted me several weeks after the fourth interview to explain that she had had an emergency appendicectomy five days after my visit and that her physical symptoms at the time could have affected some of her responses to the questions I asked.

Arguably, these signs of interviewees' involvement indicated their acceptance of the goals of the research project rather than any desire to feel themselves participating in a personal relationship with me. Yet the research was presented to them as my research in which I had a personal interest, so it is not likely that a hard and fast dividing line between the two was drawn. One index of their and my reactions to our joint participation in the repeated interviewing situation is that some four years after the final interview I am still in touch with more than a third of the women I interviewed. Four have become close friends, several others I visit occasionally, and the rest write or telephone when they have something salient to report such as the birth of another child.

Oakley, A., 'Interviewing women: a contradiction in terms', in *Doing Feminist Research,* edited by Roberts, H., Routledge and Kegan Paul, 1981

Questions

1 With reference to Readings 12, 13 and 14, what appear to be the problems inherent in the interview situation?
2 'Personal involvement in interviews, increases validity but reduced reliability.' Explain and evaluate this statement.
3 Contrast the value of using interviews with any *one* other method of social research.

11 Projects in methodology

In this final chapter we give some brief suggestions for exercises that can be undertaken to develop a fuller understanding of some of the main concepts presented in this book. A grasp of what is meant by operationalisation, what is involved in phrasing appropriate questions for a questionnaire, or the techniques of keeping an interview going in the strange territory of someone else's living room, can be best obtained by having a go. In the bibliography we mention some books that have further specific ideas for 'field projects', that can be followed up. The exercises suggested here, if tried, will do much to introduce the broad range of problems connected with research in sociology.

Project 1   Evaluating sociological research

With reference to the ideas set out in Chapter 4, choose a suitable sociological study and analyse it in terms of the various stages suggested: theory, hypothesis, operationalisation, field work and results. Not all accounts of sociological research will give details of all these stages and the framework should not be applied in an over rigid way. However, by bearing it in mind, the relationship between theory and method can be investigated, and the adequacy of the techniques used can be assessed. What this approach should enable you to do is to form a judgement about the quality of the work undertaken.

Project 2   The problem of operationalisation

Much sociological research, particularly if it is in any sense deductive, involves taking theoretical concepts and operationalising them or expressing them in such a way as to make them measurable (see Chapter 6). Take one of the following concepts and after consulting relevant references, suggest practical ways in which they may be operationalised. (The work of Blauner on *alienation*, which is summarised in many textbooks, provides a good example of this process.)

Class	'Moral Panic'	Immigrant
Community	Prejudice	Good health
Proletariat	Poverty	Leisure activity
Deviant	Unemployed	Christian

Some consideration should be given to how some of these concepts can be 'scaled' to show the degree of the factor being considered (e.g. amount of 'moral panic', relative class position, degree of prejudice, level of poverty etc.).

Project 3   Estimation of social mobility

The pattern of male social mobility in your area can be studied in a preliminary way by interviewing a sample of men between the ages of 20 and 30. As a large sample is beneficial for this exercise it may be best if it is undertaken by a whole group. The simple questionnaire schedule will need to cover a their age, b sufficient detail on their current job or last job – if any – if now unemployed, c their father's main occupation (again in sufficient details). Using a suitable reference, like the Registrar General's scale, assess the class position of the sons and their fathers. A simple table can then be constructed (see Fig. 11.1). Background

Figure 11.1 Table for estimating social mobility

Father's class position	Son's class position					
	1	2	3	4	5	6
1						
2						
3						
4						
5						
6						

Note: each son can be placed in the appropriate cell according to their current class position and their father's class. When all data is entered, percentages can be calculated.

reading for this project can be found in many textbooks which discuss Glass's study of social mobility (1954) and the Oxford Mobility Study (Halsey *et al.*, 1980).

A further exercise can be undertaken to assess female social mobility. The problem of classifying the class position of women will be highlighted by this but it is well worth giving some time and thought to the issue.

Project 4   A questionnaire

Design a short questionnaire that can be given, or posted, to respondents. The issue chosen should be one relevant to your place of study (college, school etc.) or your local community. Give special attention to overall organisation of questions and phrasing of questions. Where possible questions should be precoded. The questionnaire should be 'piloted' on a small sub-sample and altered if necessary before it is administered to your main sample.

Project 5   An interview

Much valuable experience of the various phases of the research process can be gained from conducting a few interviews. Choose any issue or social group that interests you (e.g. the elderly, the experience of unemployment, rastafarians, working in a pub etc.) and design a brief interview schedule, after having completed suitable background reading. Work in pairs and carry out the interviews using a portable tape-recorder. The results can then be transcribed (a laborious task!) or a tape made containing selected illustrative extracts. The purpose of this project is to learn the problems of interviewing by actually doing an interview. For this reason there is no need to undertake many of them. However the success or failure of different parts of your procedure (e.g. the design of your schedule, establishing rapport, operating a tape-recorder, analysing oral data etc.) should be carefully reviewed.

Project 6   A 'new experience' – an exercise in observation

Getting a 'taste' of participant observation is not particularly easy because it is not just a matter of joining in with some suitable group. The skill is to 'join in' but also to be able to maintain a degree of detachment and to sytematically analyse the experience from a sociological point of view. Nevertheless the following exercise should be of value.

Choose a 'new experience'. This should be the experience of some social situation or activity that you have never undertaken before. It need not be very exotic but it should be new to you. Some examples of the sort of activity you might think about are:

1 Going to a Turkish bath.
2 Going racing (horses or dogs).
3 Visiting a pentecostal or a spiritualist church.
4 Going to a concert (folk, pop, classical, Indian etc.) that is new to you.
5 Visiting a magistrates court.
6 Taking a ferry to France.
7 Spending some time in a betting shop.

The experience should be one where there are not serious problems of 'entry', 'gatekeepers' or 'acquiring a native costume'. As far as possible try to find out about the situation before you participate in it (by reading or asking suitable informants). Go into the observation with some broad issue that you wish to focus on; it is not enough to 'just experience'. Observe with care. Write up a detailed description as soon as possible afterwards, noting any aspect that seemed relevant and also the ways that other participants interpreted or 'made sense' of their world.

Review your research in terms of the type of knowledge you have acquired. Consider how it differs from the sort of information you would have obtained if you had carried out an interview or used a questionnaire instead.

Further reading

There are many detailed books on methodology in sociology currently available. The books listed below are considered readable and of value for study or reference purposes on introductory courses. The specific research studies already discussed in the text are implicitly recommended as examples of different research techniques. Details of these books have already been given.

Ackroyd, S., and Hughes, J.A., *Data Collection in Context*, Longman, 1981.
    After a general introduction to the problems of data collection and social theory, the social survey, interviewing and participant observation are looked at in detail.
Bell, C., and Newby, H., eds., *Doing Sociological Research*, George Allen and Unwin, 1977.
    A useful 'reader' with a number of contributors reflecting on the problems they faced doing their research. The accounts are relevant to the kind of issues raised in this book.
Bell, C., and Roberts, H., eds., *Social Researching*, Routledge and Kegan Paul, 1984.
    Another 'reader' in which sociologists reflect on the 'politics, problems and practice' involved in research they have carried out.
Berger, P., and Kellner, H., *Sociology Reinterpreted*, Penguin, 1982.
    While not a methodology book as such, an entertaining account is provided of an interpretive approach to what constitutes sociological inquiry and evidence.
Broad, W., and Wade, N., *Betrayers of the Truth*, Simon and Schuster, 1982.
    An unusual and highly readable book about the scientific method which suggests that science is much more open to fraud and 'fiddling' than is generally realised.
Bulmer, M., ed., *Sociological Research Methods*, Macmillan, 1977.
    Detailed reference book with a variety of contributors on most aspects of the research process.

Burgess, R., ed., *Field Research: A Sourcebook and Field Manual*, George Allen and Unwin, 1982.

　　The field research tradition is extensively covered in this reader; sections include: sampling, field roles and field problems, conversations in the field, historical sources and recording field data.

Gomm, R., and McNeill, P., *Handbook for Sociology Teachers*, Heinemann Educational Books, 1982.

　　Many helpful suggestions for little research projects along with other ideas for introductory sociology courses.

Hoinville, G., Jowell, R., *et al.*, *Survey Research Practice*, Heinemann Educational Books, 1977.

　　A guide for researchers covering practical problems from constructing questionnaires and interviewing to sampling and doing fieldwork.

Hughes, J., *The Philosophy of Social Research*, Longman, 1980.

　　As the title suggests this book looks at the theoretical issues in methodology; there is a useful discussion of positivism, the humanist approach, meaning and social research.

Pratt, V., *The Philosophy of the Social Sciences*, Methuen, 1978.

　　The social sciences are set in a philosophical context in this book with numerous short chapters ranging over a wide variety of issues; particularly useful on the scientific method and the nature of sociological knowledge.

Rose, G., *Deciphering Sociological Research*, Macmillan, 1982.

　　An imaginative approach to the problem of making sense of other people's research. The chapters on the various aspects of research are backed up well with detailed accounts of contrasting research projects.

Roberts, H., *Doing Feminist Research*, Routledge and Kegan Paul, 1981.

　　Another 'reader', but this time looking at the problems associated with research by and about women; many valuable practical examples given.

Index

alienation study 30
analytic induction method 95
anthropology 43, 45
    and myths 96, 97

Belfast research 52
biology 24, 26
Box, S. 77, 78

Cartesian theory 24
Census 13
childbirth research 92, 99–101
children through to adulthood,
    research 13, 14
class hierarchy: life chances 16
cluster sampling 33, 34
coding in questionnaires 39
Cornerville research 46, 49, 50
crime and statistics 77, 78
'cuffing' 77, 80, 81

Darwinian theory 23
data,
    analysis 64
    interpretation of 60
    qualitative 66
    recording of 53, 54, 60
deviance,
    research 91
    statistics 78, 79
    see also Humphreys, Laud
Durkheim, Emile 20, 26, 68, 69, 77, 89

embourgeoisement thesis 30
empiricism 17, 20, 87, 88
epistemology 19
ethics, of research 54, 55
ethnographic method 83, 91
evolution theory 23

Festinger, L. 45, 47
Feyerabend 24, 25
field studies,
    and research 60, 64–66
    tradition 43, 45
    see also participant observation
functionalism 26, 27

Gaia hypothesis 24
gang activity 1, 2, 4, 9, 31
gender thesis 30
General Household Survey 13, 35, 91
general universe sample 31
Gouldner, A. 74, 91
grounded theory 30, 84, 89, 90

Heisenberg 25, 26, 28
historicist theory 21
Humphreys, Laud 45, 46, 48, 53, 55,
    56, 67

'ideal type' 70, 71
indictable offences 4
    and statistics 3, 4, 80
inductive method 17
interpretive approach 27, 28, 35, 91, 92
interviews,
    problems of 53, 92–101
    project 105–6
    specific 93–101
    technique in 41, 42, 53
    unstructured 11

Kuhn, T. 22, 23, 28

logico-deductive theory 90

'McIver, Mrs' 93, 94
macrosociology, defined 10
    and, positivism 27
    research 11, 58, 65
    social structure 14, 15
marihuana research 16, 91, 95, 96
market research 35
Marx, Karl, critics of 21, 29
    and, economic objectivity 69, 70

empiricism 88
macrosociology 10, 29
materialism 87–89
positivism 20, 27, 88
radical sociology 16, 27
Marxist analysis 15, 84
ideology 86, 87
theory 83, 84
Mead, Margaret 43, 92, 96, 97
methodology, in research 58, 84–86
and theory 14
value freedom 69–71
microsociology, defined 9
and grounded theory 30
interpretive approach 27
research 10, 12, 59
social action 14, 15
middle level theory 30
mobility research 13
multi-stage sampling 34

NASA 24
National Opinion Poll 75, 77, 78
newspapers and research 7
novels and research 4, 5

objectivity in the sciences 68, 69
observation, see participant
ontology 19
operationalisation project 102–3
opiate drugs, use of 16, 91, 95, 96
opportunity sample 34

parapsychology 11
participant observation and data
recording 53, 54
ethical issues 54, 55
interviewing 53
methods 44
models for 45–47
oral histories 56
project 106–7
research 4, 11, 28, 43, 44, 85
researchers difficulties 48–52
sampling 48
path analysis 64
physics 23, 24
pilot study 37, 38
politics 73
and statistics 76, 77

polls and statistics 75, 77, 78
population sample 31
positivism 20, 26–28, 92
poverty, culture of 30
prisons 31

qualitative research, defined 10–12, 16
evaluated 67
see also participant observation
Quantum theory 23
quantitative research, defined 13, 14
examples 61–65
model 58, 59
structural approach 16
use of 30
questionnaries 36, 37
and, coding 38, 39
construction of 38–41
interviewing 41
postal 41
project 104–5
questions in surveys 35, 63
informed 53
reliability of 36, 37
validity of 36
quota sampling 35

research, hypotheses 60, 62, 64
methods and theory 14, 28–30,
83–86
and operationalism 60, 62
process, elements of 57–60;
evaluation of 61, 66
results 60, 64

Samoan research 92, 96, 97
sampling, methods used 33–35, 60, 66
selection for 32
types of 31–34, 48
schools and research 83
streaming 9
statistics 76, 77
sciences (natural), aspects of 19
definitions of 17, 68, 69
methods in 18–22
and objectivity 22, 23, 25, 68, 72
revolutions in 22
and social survey 17
and sociology 19, 20, 24, 25
self-fulfilling prophecy 29

social action, definition 14, 16
society, primary understanding 5–7
spoonbending 11, 12, 25, 47
Stanleyville research 49, 51, 52
statistics, critique of 77–79
    production of 75, 76
structural approach 14, 16
suicide 26, 27, 69, 77
surveys and interviews 41
    positivism 27
    sampling 32
    science 17
    see also questions
symbolic interaction 27, 85

'tearoom trade' *see* Humphreys, Laud
Tepotzlan study 57, 58

theory and methodology 14, 15, 29,
    84–86
    research 29, 30, 57, 58

value freedom 28, 68–71, 74

Weber, Max, and bureaucracy 89
    'ideal type' 70, 71
    macrosociology 10
    microsociology 27
    social action 27, 86
    value freedom 28, 70, 71
'white-collar work' research 61–65
Whyte, W. F. 35, 46, 49, 50, 54, 67
'wife's' interview 97–99
women interviewed 99–101